DANIEL

ABINGDON OLD TESTAMENT COMMENTARIES

DANIEL

DONALD E. GOWAN

Abingdon Press
Nashville

ABINGDON OLD TESTAMENT COMMENTARIES
DANIEL

Copyright © 2001 by Abingdon Press

This book is printed on recycled, acid-free, elemental-chlorine–free paper.

Library of Congress Cataloging-in-Publication Data

Gowan, Donald E.
   Daniel / Donald E. Gowan.
     p. cm.—(Abingdon Old Testament commentaries)
   Includes bibliographical references and index.
   ISBN 0-687-08421-0 (alk. paper)
   1. Bible. O.T. Daniel—Criticism, interpretation, etc. I. Title. II. Series.

BS1555.52 .G69 2001
224'.507—dc21

                   2001027949

Scripture quotations, unless otherwise noted, are from the New Revised Standard Version of the Bible, copyright © 1989, by the Division of Christian Education of the National Council of the Churches of Christ in the United States of America. Used by permission.

Those noted KJV are from the King James Version.

Scripture quotations marked (CEV) are from the Contemporary English Version. Copyright © 1991, 1992, 1995 by American Bible Society. Used by permission.

01 02 03 04 05 06 07 08 09 10—10 9 8 7 6 5 4 3 2 1

MANUFACTURED IN THE UNITED STATES OF AMERICA

CONTENTS

FOREWORD

The *Abingdon Old Testament Commentaries* are offered to the reader in hopes that they will aid in the study of Scripture and provoke a deeper understanding of the Bible in all its many facets. The texts of the Old Testament come out of a time, a language, and socio-historical and religious circumstances far different from the present. Yet Jewish and Christian communities have held to them as a sacred canon, significant for faith and life in each new time. Only as one engages these books in depth and with all the critical and intellectual faculties available to us, can the contemporary communities of faith and other interested readers continue to find them meaningful and instructive.

These volumes are designed and written to provide compact, critical commentaries on the books of the Old Testament for the use of theological students and pastors. It is hoped that they may be of service also to upper-level college or university students and to those responsible for teaching in congregational settings. In addition to providing basic information and insights into the Old Testament writings, these commentaries exemplify the tasks and procedures of careful interpretation.

The writers of the commentaries in this series come from a broad range of ecclesiastical affiliations, confessional stances, and educational backgrounds. They have experience as teachers and, in some instances, as pastors and preachers. In most cases, the authors are persons who have done significant research on the book that is their assignment. They take full account of the most important current scholarship and secondary literature, while not attempting to summarize that literature or to engage in technical academic debate. The fundamental concern of each volume is analysis and discussion of the literary, socio-historical, theological, and ethical dimensions of the biblical texts themselves.

The New Revised Standard Version of the Bible is the principal translation of reference for the series, though authors may draw upon other interpretations in their discussion. Each writer is attentive to the original Hebrew text in preparing the commentary. But the authors do not presuppose any knowledge of the biblical languages on the part of the reader. When some awareness of a grammatical, syntactical, or philological issue is necessary for an adequate understanding of a particular text, the issue is explained simply and concisely.

Each volume consists of four parts. An *introduction* looks at the book as a whole to identify *key issues* in the book, its *literary genre* and *structure*, the *occasion and situational context* of the book (including both social and historical contexts), and the *theological and ethical* significance of the book.

The *commentary* proper organizes the text by literary units and, insofar as is possible, divides the comment into three parts. The *literary analysis* serves to introduce the passage with particular attention to identification of the genre of speech or literature and the structure or outline of the literary unit under discussion. Here also, the author takes up significant stylistic features to help the reader understand the mode of communication and its impact on comprehension and reception of the text. The largest part of the comment is usually found in the *exegetical analysis*, which considers the leading concepts of the unit, the language of expression, and problematical words, phrases, and ideas in order to get at the aim or intent of the literary unit, as far as that can be uncovered. Attention is given here to particular historical and social situations of the writer(s) and reader(s) where that is discernible and relevant as well as to wider cultural (including religious) contexts. The analysis does not proceed phrase by phrase or verse by verse but deals with the various particulars in a way that keeps in view the overall structure and central focus of the passage and its relationship to the general line of thought or rhetorical argument of the book as a whole. The final section, *theological and ethical analysis* seeks to identify and clarify the theological and ethical matters with which the unit deals or to which it points. Though not aimed primarily at contemporary issues of faith and life, this section should provide readers a basis for reflection on them.

Each volume also contains a select bibliography of works cited in the commentary as well as major commentaries and other important works available in English. A subject index is provided to help the reader get at matters that cut across different texts.

The fundamental aim of this series will have been attained if readers are assisted not only to understand more about the origins, character, and meaning of the Old Testament writings, but also to enter into their own informed and critical engagement with the texts themselves.

Patrick D. Miller
General Editor

INTRODUCTION

THE INTERPRETATION OF DANIEL

The book of Daniel has attracted probably a greater variety of interpretations than any other biblical book. Studying the history of its interpretation thus introduces one to many of the issues that have arisen in the exposition of Scripture during the past two millennia. The book also serves well as a source of examples of virtually every aspect of contemporary biblical scholarship. A tremendous volume of literature has been produced on Daniel, so a brief survey such as this can choose only a limited number of examples to illustrate the variety of ways the book has been used.

Daniel does not claim to be a prophet, and except for the fact that both he and some of the Old Testament prophets record their experiences of visions, the book does not use the genres that are typical of the prophetic books. In spite of this, the earliest references to the book speak of him as a prophet. A fragmentary manuscript from Cave 4 at Qumran contains a few words from Dan 11:32 and 12:10, attributing them to "Daniel the prophet" (Allegro 1968, 54-55), and Matt 24:15 uses the same expression with reference to the "desolating sacrilege" (alluding to Dan 11:31; 12:11). A Jewish document of the first century AD, *The Lives of the Prophets*, includes a section on Daniel, and at the end of the century Josephus called him "one of the greatest of the prophets" (*Antiquities of the Jews*, 10.11.4, sec. 266). It needs to be kept in mind, with reference to later debates over the character of the book, that "prophet" was used at this time in a very broad sense, of any person considered to have been inspired (note Peter's designation of David as a prophet in Acts 2:30). The prophetic books were not read for insight into their work with Israel of their own times, but were of interest as predictions of the future; and since this book could be seen to contain very accurate predictions, it seemed to belong in their company. In the Greek translation of the Old Testament (the Septuagint), the book was included with the prophets, and that has influenced the Christian understanding of the book until modern times.

Except for "shut the mouths of lions, quenched raging fire" in Heb 11:33*b*-34*a*, the stories in Daniel 1–6 were not used by the New Testament writers, but the visions and Nebuchadnezzar's dream in chapter 2 played an important role in the development of New Testament thought. The term "Son of Man," which Jesus used of himself, has clear associations with Daniel 7 (Matt 24:30; 26:64; Mark 8:38; 13:26; 14:62; Luke 21:27). "Kingdom of God," which plays a major role in Jesus' teachings, is a term that seldom appears in the Old Testament, but the imminent coming of an eternal kingdom is a prominent theme in Daniel (2:44; 4:3, 34; 6:26; 7:14, 27). The "desolating sacrilege" (Matt 24:15; Mark 13:14; Dan 11:31; 12:11) has already been alluded to, and Paul's reference to the archenemy of the future in 2 Thess 2:4 sounds like an echo of Dan 11:36. The only Old Testament parallel to the frequent New Testament references to resurrection for reward and punishment appears in Dan 12:2. The angels Gabriel (Luke 1:19, 26) and Michael (Jude 9; Rev 12:7) appear in the Old Testament only in Daniel (8:16; 9:21; and 10:13, 21; 12:1). There are more than sixty parallels between Daniel and Revelation, too many to begin to cite here. It will be noted that it was the eschatological passages of Daniel that attracted the attention of the New Testament writers.

In contrast to the Christian uses of Daniel in the first century, Jewish texts found the stories of faithfulness under persecution to speak most directly to them. As early as about 100 BC, 1 Macc 2:60 referred to the fiery furnace and the den of lions, and the same allusions reappear in 3 Macc 6:7 (late first century BC) and 4 Macc 16:3, 21; 18:12-13 (first century AD). Josephus retold the stories of chapters 1–6 but used only one of the visions (Dan 8).

Two apocalyptic works from the end of the first century AD make use of Daniel, as might be expected. Second Esdras 12:11 reinterprets the fourth kingdom as Rome, and 2 *Baruch* 36–40 used the four-empire scheme in the same way.

Since it is the visions of Daniel that have drawn the greatest attention (and the most varying interpretations) over the centuries, one way of summarizing briefly the ways the book has been read is to consider what period of history the interpreter believes Daniel is referring to in his predictions. This enables us to outline four ways of reading the book, and a few examples of each approach will be offered. These widely differing conclusions have been reached because of disagreements over the identity of the fourth empire in chapters 2 and 7, the identity of the stone in chapter 2 and the eternal kingdom of chapters 2 and 7, the identity of the archtyrant who appears in chapters 7, 8, 9, and 11, and the proper way to understand the various numbers: "time, two times, and half a time" (7:25); 2,300 evenings and mornings (8:14); 70 weeks of years (9:24-27), 1,290 days (12:11) and 1,335 days (12:12).

The four periods that have been proposed as the time for the culmination of history that Daniel refers to are (1) the second century BC; (2) the first century AD; (3) a future time distant from the interpreter's present; and (4) the interpreter's near future:

1. The climax occurs with the demise of Antiochus IV Epiphanes, who persecuted the Jews in the mid–second century BC. The first author to propose this reading was Porphyry, an opponent of Christianity who in the late third century AD claimed that the book was not prophecy written in the sixth century but was produced at the time of Antiochus IV. This view was challenged by Jerome in his commentary (late fourth century), and found little favor until the rise of historical-critical scholarship in the nineteenth century. It is the view advocated in this commentary, as in most contemporary commentaries. The fourth empire is thus identified with the Hellenistic kingdoms that succeeded Alexander, and the archtyrant is Antiochus IV. The eternal kingdom represents a hope for the Jews who remain faithful under persecution, and the numbers are to be associated with the period

of approximately three years during which Antiochus attempted to wipe out the Jewish faith (167–164 BC).

2. The fourth empire is Rome, and the climax is the coming of Jesus Christ. A variation finds both the first and second advents in the book. In the second century AD, Justin Martyr found evidence for the virgin birth in Daniel's term "one like a Son of Man" (7:13) and in the stone "cut out, not by human hands" (2:34). In the second century AD, Irenaeus (d. 195) identified the stone with the first advent and the coming of the Son of Man on the clouds with the second. The archtyrant he identified with the antichrist who will appear at the time of the consummation. Others, such as Jerome (345–413) and Augustine (354–430) were willing to associate the stone that filled the whole earth with the church. Much later, Calvin read Daniel in a strongly historical way, finding the enemies to be primarily Rome (chaps. 2 and 7) and Antiochus IV (chap. 8), rather than the pope or Muhammad, who had become favorite candidates for the archtyrant by the sixteenth century.

3. Some of those who have identified the fourth kingdom as Rome have used Daniel as evidence that the end time was to come in their near future (see 4, below), but others have not used the book in that way. For example, Hippolytus (c. 170–235) , a disciple of Irenaeus and the author of the earliest known commentary on Daniel, calculated the time of the end in an imaginative way: Christ was born five thousand five hundred years after creation, and since for God one day equals a thousand years, six thousand years must be accomplished that the Sabbath may come. Hippolytus thus thought the millennium would begin five hundred years after the time of Christ, long after his own time. Major scholars such as Jerome, Augustine, and Aquinas showed little interest in estimating the time of the end, and the same was true of Calvin during the Reformation. All contemporary scholarship, including some of the most conservative, also understands that it is inappropriate to try to use Daniel to set dates.

4. Various ingenious ways have been devised to make Daniel appear to be a book that speaks of the interpreter's own time, and to promise that the consummation is near. When the Islamic armies began to threaten Europe, both Jewish and Christian com-

mentators identified the fourth empire with Islam. Luther was influenced by calculations prevalent in his time, similar to those used long before by Hippolytus but resulting in expectations focusing on the date 1530. At that time, Luther published a translation of Daniel with a long preface expressing his conviction that the end was near.

In seventeenth-century England, during the rule of the Puritans, a group known as the Fifth Monarchy Men claimed to be the saints of Dan 7:18, and during their short-lived career predicted that Cromwell's rule would come to an end after three and one-half years (in 1657; Towner 1983, 46-63). In American history, the most sensational example of date-setting based on Daniel occurred in the mid–nineteenth century. William Miller took 457 BC to be the date when Artaxerxes I commissioned Ezra to return to Jerusalem (Ezra 7:1), and identified this date with the going forth of a word "to restore and rebuild Jerusalem" in Dan 9:25. Assuming that days in Daniel equal years (as others have done), he then added the number 2,300, from Dan 8:14, to 457 BC and concluded that the Second Coming could be expected in AD 1843. He convinced large numbers of people, and when nothing happened in 1843, he recalculated and announced a specific date, October 22, 1844 (Festinger, Riecken, and Schachter 1956, 12-23). His failure did not bring to an end this sort of misuse of Daniel (and Revelation) in American Christianity, however. Since this is the sort of use of the book that most Americans are likely to encounter in religious television and popular religious books, a brief description of two such ways of using the book will be offered here, and the commentary will occasionally explain why they are inappropriate.

For those who are convinced that Daniel speaks of our own time, the fact that it literally leads only to the time of Antiochus IV, or at best to the first-century Roman Empire, must be overcome somehow. One effort, which has been called the "futurist school," emphasizes continuity, claiming the European nations down to the present really represent the continuation of the Roman Empire. So we are still in the fourth empire period. For some who advocate this approach the fact that the European Common Market once was composed of ten nations seemed obviously to be the fulfillment of the ten horns in Dan 7:7. But now the European Union has more than ten nations!

The approach called "dispensationalism" claims there is a gap between Dan 9:26a and 9:26b, and corresponding verses elsewhere, such as 11:39 and 11:40. The text takes us to the time of Christ in chapter 9, or of Antiochus in chapter 11, then without warning skips to the end time, which lies in our immediate future (as if nothing that happened between then and now was of any importance to God). In commenting on Daniel, numerous examples of efforts to make a book of the Bible say what one wants it to say will be noted, but none is more obvious than this. Most commentators do not refer to such misuses of the book, but the reader is reminded of them here because they are such a prominent part of American culture.

THE ORIGINS OF THE BOOK OF DANIEL

The Historical Setting of the Book

The book is set in Babylonia and Persia during the sixth century BC; but while some of its information concerning this period is accurate, several details have raised questions about the actual date (or dates) of its composition. In 605 BC, Nabopolassar, king of Babylonia, died, and his son Nebuchadnezzar acceded to the throne. According to Jer 25:1, the first year of Nebuchadnezzar was the fourth year of Jehoiakim, king of Judah. Daniel 1:1-2 says that Nebuchadnezzar attacked Jerusalem and took away exiles and spoils in Jehoiakim's third year, however. There is no record elsewhere of such an event, in the Bible or the Babylonian Chronicle (Grayson 1975a, 102), both of which indicate that Jerusalem fell to Nebuchadnezzar for the first time in 597 BC. (For efforts to explain this, see the commentary on Dan 1.) The book thus raises a historical question at the very beginning.

Chapters 1–5 and 7–8 are set in the Neo-Babylonian period. They contain some accurate details for that period, but tend to speak in general terms of court life as it might have been found throughout the ancient Near East. One problem with historicity must be dealt with in the commentary on chapter 5. Belshazzar was not the son of Nebuchadnezzar and was never called king in the Babylonian records, but served only as regent for a time. The sequence of Neo-Babylonian kings after Nebuchadnezzar was as follows: Amel-Marduk (561–559), Nergal-shar-usur (559–555), Labashi-marduk (555), then the usurper Nabonidus (555–539). Belshazzar was the son of Nabonidus.

The city of Babylon was taken over by the Persians in 539, and this leads to another problem in the book of Daniel, which says the city fell to "Darius the Mede." Chapters 6 and 9 are dated in his reign, but no such figure has been found in any of the texts from the ancient Near East, and indeed there is no place in history for the reign of such a person. Nabonidus was succeeded immediately by Cyrus the Persian, who is the last king to be named in Daniel (1:21 and 10:1). The problem of Darius the Mede will be discussed in the commentary on chapter 6.

The coming of Alexander the Great into the Middle East is recorded in cryptic terms in 8:5, 21 and 11:3 (333–323 BC). Chapter 11 then tells the history of the rule of Ptolemies (kings of Egypt, called "king of the south") and Seleucids (kings of Syria and Mesopotamia, called "king of the north") until the time of the persecution of the Jews by the Seleucid king Antiochus IV Epiphanes. All the names can be supplied for the anonymous figures in the chapter, from extrabiblical sources, and the author knew the history in detail from about 260 to 165 BC. The author accurately refers to two campaigns Antiochus led against Egypt, but then speaks of a third, after which Antiochus was to die on the coast of Palestine (11:40-45). This did not happen. He led his army to Parthia instead, finally decided to rescind the decree proscribing Judaism, and died soon after. The book of Daniel shows no knowledge of any of this.

The inaccuracies in the stories set in the Neo-Babylonian period, the great accuracy of the account of the affairs of the Ptolemies and Seleucids up to a point near the end of the life of Antiochus IV, and the mistaken prediction of his death, have led contemporary scholars to a conclusion about the date of the final form of the book.

The Date of the Book

The date of Daniel became a matter of great controversy in the nineteenth century. Many scholars began to agree with Porphyry, that the book was not written in the sixth century BC but in the second. This seemed to make it a fraudulent work, given the modern assumptions about authorship. E. B. Pusey began his 1868 defense of the traditional view of the book with these impassioned words:

> The book of Daniel is especially fitted to be a battlefield between faith and unbelief. It admits of no half-measures. It is either Divine or an imposture. To write any book under the name of another, and to give it out to be his, is, in any case, a forgery, dishonest in itself, and destructive of all trustworthiness. (Pusey 1868, 1)

The question of authorship will be discussed in the next section. The sixth-century date continues to have defenders, but the commentary will show that the efforts to explain the apparent historical errors in chapters 1–6, especially those concerning Belshazzar and Darius the Mede have not been found to be adequate, as most scholars evaluate them. If the book was completed just before the death of Antiochus, the features that have been noted above are easy to understand. When the author writes of the distant past, Neo-Babylonian and Persian periods, he is sometimes accurate, sometimes not, depending on the resources available to him. Memory or written record of the recent past, the hellenistic period, enables him to describe it very accurately. When he speaks of his own actual future, he usually does so in very general terms (as in 2:44-45; 7:26-27; 8:25b; 9:27b); and when he does get specific (11:40-45), he has no more exact knowledge of the future than any other human being—inspired or not. So Daniel can be dated more closely than any other biblical book, in 165 BC.

These discussions have referred to the completion of the book and do not necessarily account for the entire history of its composition. Scholars have argued that it was all written in the second century, but current opinion tends toward dating the visions of chapters 7–12 then and looking to an earlier period for the origin of chapters 1–6. This might account for the early and Eastern features of the Aramaic of chapters 2–6 (Collins 1993, 13-17; Polak 1993, 249-65), but the principal reason for the early dating is the different attitude toward the kings in chapters 1–6 and 7–12. The king in the first half of the book is an oriental potentate with great power and with whims to be feared, but he is basically a reasonable man whose mind can be (and is) changed. Darius the Mede is even a great friend of Daniel, who greatly regrets being tricked into having to condemn him to the lions' den. In contrast, the foreign king in chapters 7–12 is the personification of evil, irredeemable, and irresistible apart from divine intervention. The stories seem to reflect a time and place when the Jews were living under reasonably peaceful circumstances, even though ruled by a foreign power. Chapters 1, 3, and 6, especially, make it clear that Jews are likely to find themselves in jeopardy at times because of the distinctive features of their religion. They reflect a certain optimism, however, about the possibility of success for talented and faithful Jews, even in the service of a pagan king. No such optimism appears in the visions, all of which are dominated by the specter of persecution. It seems likely, then, that the stories took essentially their present form before persecution began, perhaps late in the Persian or early in the hellenistic period.

Authorship and the Question of Pseudonymity

The first six chapters are stories about Daniel, speaking of him in the third person, and so are anonymous as to authorship. Daniel speaks in the first person in chapters 7–12, and since he dates his visions in the reigns of Belshazzar and Cyrus, the traditional view has been that this sixth-century character was responsible for the whole book. There may well have been a Daniel in exile around whom these legends grew up, although we know nothing more about him. Other occurrences of the name seem to refer to an ancient Daniel (or Danel), rather than the hero of the Exile. Ezekiel refers to Noah, Daniel, and Job in Ezek 14:14, 20; Noah and Job were famous characters from the distant past, while the Daniel of our book would have been a younger contemporary of Ezekiel. He also compares the wisdom of the king of Tyre to that of Daniel in 28:3, and in all three cases the consonantal text reads "Danel" rather than "Daniel." *Jubilees* 4:20 speaks of a Danel who was uncle and father-in-law of Enoch. Perhaps Ezekiel knew of legends about him that are lost to us. The Ugaritic texts also contain references to a Danel, who is known for his kindness to widows and orphans ("The Tale of Aqhat," Pritchard 1955, 149-55). If the stories about Daniel of the Exile did exist earlier than the second century, then claiming a second-century date for the visions and the final form of the book means we are postulating that an anonymous author who wrote during the persecution added his visions to the stories and attributed them to the exilic hero.

Given modern conceptions of authorship, this seems fraudulent, but it is important not to impose our understandings on people of the past. In the ancient Near East most works of literature were anonymous, and there was no concern with "intellectual property." People did not earn money from the sale of their writings, and the notion of copyright is a very modern idea. By the second century BC it had become a standard practice to ascribe one's work to a famous figure from the past; to Enoch, Abraham, Solomon, Baruch, or Ezra, for example. If the author of this book was not the Daniel of the Exile, then, he was not doing something irregular for that time, but was only following a common practice. Numerous theories to explain the reason for the practice have been proposed; perhaps it is enough to suggest that when an author had something important to convey, it seemed appropriate to say it in the name of a respected character from the past (Russell 1964, 127-39).

Language and Text

One of the mysteries of the book is the fact that it divides into two parts in two different ways. The division by literary type into stories and visions has already been noted. It is also approximately half in Hebrew and half in Aramaic, but chapters 1–2:4*a* and 8–12 are in Hebrew and 2:4*b*–7:28 in Aramaic—one of six stories in Hebrew, one of four visions in Aramaic. The language changes early in the second story with the word "Aramaic" appearing in the middle of 2:4. The reader is not alerted to the change back to Hebrew between chapters 7 and 8.

There has been debate over whether the original language was one or the other, accompanied by theories of partial translation to account for the present situation, but it is hard to explain why a book would have been partially translated in this way. A fairly complicated recent description of its origin may be as convincing as any (Collins 1993, 24-38). Earliest are the stories in chapters 2–6, written in Aramaic. The original language of the visions in 8–12 was Hebrew, and the vision in chapter 7 was written in Aramaic in order to connect the two parts of the book. Finally, chapter 1 was written in Hebrew as an introduction to the book.

The text has for the most part been well preserved in spite of its unusual character, and there are few extremely difficult translation problems. The translator does have to deal with an unusual number of rare words, especially loan-words from Persian. In chapter 3 there even appear a few words borrowed from Greek, as the commentary on the chapter will note. There exists a significant number of variants between the Masoretic text and the two ancient Greek translations that are extant. The earliest translation, now called the Old Greek, is available in only a few manuscripts, since it was replaced in the Septuagint at an early period by Theodotion's version. The Old Greek preserves significantly different versions of chapters 4 and 5, evidence for two early traditions as to how those stories should be told. Detailed studies of the Greek texts may be found in thorough commentaries such as those by Montgomery, Goldingay, and Collins.

Place in the Canon

No author in early Judaism or Christianity questioned the inspiration and authority of Daniel, and it has been noted that he was considered to be a prophet. In Judaism, with its custom of copying works of Scripture on scrolls, a Daniel scroll would not necessarily have a fixed place with reference to other scrolls, but the church's copies of the Septuagint were in codex (book) form, and they located Daniel with the prophetic books. Eventually, Judaism located the book in the third section of the canon, however: the Writings, between Esther and Ezra.

A more important difference between church and synagogue is

to be found in the addition of materials known to us only in Greek. The book is preceded in the Septuagint (but included as chapter 13 in Roman Catholic translations of the Old Testament) by Susanna, a brief story of a young woman falsely accused of adultery and saved by Daniel's clever cross-examination of the accusers. The story of Shadrach, Meshach, and Abednego in Dan 3 is expanded between verses 23 and 24 of the Aramaic text by the Prayer of Azariah and the Song of the Three Jews. Following the book are two short stories called Bel and the Dragon. Since these were not to be found in the Jewish scriptures consulted by the Reformers, they were included with the other Old Testament books known only in Greek, and printed separately in Protestant Bibles as the Apocrypha. This commentary deals only with the Hebrew/Aramaic book.

DANIEL AS A WORK OF LITERATURE

There are two major genres in the book, as already noted—story and vision-account. Within each of them may be found other short genres. Awareness of the special qualities of these two types of literature, as they are used in Daniel, will add to the appreciation of the book.

The Genres in Daniel 1–6

Older commentaries, and more recent works by the most conservative scholars (Young 1949; Miller 1994), take the stories in chapters 1–6 to be historical reports and show no interest in similar stories elsewhere. Before the development of form criticism, however, it was already noticed that the stories in Daniel had parallels in Gen 41 and the story of Ahiqar (Barton 1899/1900, 242-47). Form criticism, enlightened by studies of folklore, identifies common patterns of speech containing important themes associated with frequently occurring life-situations. Those patterns then reappear in a variety of written works, varied to suit the purposes of the particular composition, without necessarily being the result of direct borrowing from another author's work. There is now evidence that this is the appropriate way to understand the relationships among the stories in Daniel, and those between Daniel and other ancient literature.

The plots of these stories show that they may be divided into two groups of three each (chaps. 1, 3, 6 and 2, 4, 5). Humphreys introduced the terms "tales of court conflict" (Dan 3 and 6) and "tales of court contests" (Dan 4 and 5) as the way to distinguish them (Humphreys 1973, 211-23). In the former, one faction seeks the ruin of another; in the latter, the hero succeeds where all others fail. His terms were useful but could be improved on, and he did not provide a careful analysis of the structure of the two types, or extensive comparison with other stories (Niditch and Doran 1977, 179-93).

There is a group of stories in the Old Testament and related literature in which wisdom plays a key role, and each of them not only has the same structure but also deals with the same issue: "Who has true wisdom?" (Gowan 1992, 85-96). Daniel 2, 4, and 5 belong with this group. We then may note that there is another theme that appears in chapters 1, 3, and 6 and may be found elsewhere as well, in a smaller group of stories, all of them Yahwistic. It deals with those who find themselves in jeopardy because of faithfulness to their religion but are delivered from the danger that threatens them. It is related to the theme described in studies of folklore as "the disgrace and rehabilitation of a minister of the court."

1. *The Wisdom Story.* The plot, repeated in Gen 41, Dan 2, 4, and 5, and elsewhere with variations, as will be shown, is as follows: All the wise men in a Gentile court are unable to explain a dream or omen that has appeared to the king. But a Jew, to whom has been given superior wisdom by his God, is able to do so and is promoted to a high position because of it, while the superiority of his God is recognized by the pagan king. Genesis 41 and Dan 2, 4, and 5 need not be retold at this point, for the exactness of the fit is obvious, but some other examples of the pattern should be helpful.

That this was a favorite theme in the Middle East is shown by the ways it occurs elsewhere. The story of the wise man Ahiqar

(Conybeare, Harris, and Lewis 1913) combines both of our themes and is introduced by the second, in order to account for his appearance as an outsider at the moment of crisis (an essential part of the wisdom story). The crisis is provoked by the request from the king of Egypt to the king of Assyria that he send someone to build him a castle in the air. Here is the impossible request that also appears in Dan 2: when Nebuchadnezzar demands that the sages tell him what he had dreamed. In these stories such requests must be taken seriously. The stories are really about contests of wits—who is the cleverest (that is, the wisest)? To respond "Please be reasonable" would mean one had lost. What is required is a clever answer, but the Assyrian king's wise men are stumped. The unsuccessful counselors are another essential part of the plot, in order to emphasize the wisdom of the outsider who succeeds. The outsider, in this case Ahiqar, is sent to Egypt with a caravan of gifts and is banqueted and tested by the Egyptian wise men until finally he must build the castle in the air. He attaches long ropes to a large basket, to which he has harnessed two great eagles. Into the basket go two small boys; the eagles are allowed to carry the basket into the air, where they hover, kept from flying away by the long ropes. The boys then call down to the pharaoh as they have been instructed: "More bricks, more bricks!" Given the rules of the game, if the pharaoh is left without a clever comeback, he has lost; the pharaoh admits it, praising Ahiqar as indeed the wisest of all men.

Each of these stories involves a king as central figure, a serious dilemma that cannot be resolved by those whose wisdom normally suffices, and an outsider of some sort who resolves it not by any significant action but by superior wisdom. The earliest known version of this basic plot appears in a fragmentary papyrus written in the thirteenth century BC (Pritchard 1955, 231-32). It reports a letter from King Apophis, who ruled the Egyptian delta, to King Seqnen-Re at Thebes insisting that King Seqnen-Re get rid of the hippopotamus pool in his city, since the noise (from four hundred miles away!) was keeping King Apophis awake. Once we note the impossible request, we expect that Seqnen-Re will call in his counselors, who will be unable to come up with the kind of answer this sort of story requires; and that is the way the papyrus continues. Then the papyrus breaks off, but the pattern is so familiar to those who know the ancient literature that the translator, John A. Wilson, suggested in a note that Seqnen-Re must have responded with "a proposition which counterchecked the problem set by the Hyksos king."

In 1 Esdr 3–4, King Darius cannot sleep, not as serious a dilemma as in the other stories but important to the king. He calls his guardsmen to entertain him through the night by coming up with the cleverest answer to his riddling question, "What is the strongest?" Each gives a good answer, but the fourth (who is a Jew, Zerubbabel) gives a double answer that outshines the others; he is suitably rewarded.

The book of Job may be read as a creative use of the same pattern. Job is not a king, but is the greatest of all the men of the east and is compared to a king. His dilemma is critical: the loss of everything, including his health. The issue throughout the dialogue is the question "Where shall wisdom be found?" His so-called friends claim they have it, but for Job they fill the role of the unsuccessful counselors. Then Elihu appears, the outsider, claiming to be the one who possesses true wisdom, as in the familiar plot. Readers would expect a satisfactory resolution with his appearance, since the pattern was so familiar; but at this point the author shatters the wisdom story, for Elihu has nothing new to contribute. Then Yahweh speaks, an utterly new and unexpected element.

The only other stories in the Old Testament in which wisdom plays any role are partly related to the pattern, but since each differs significantly they will not be retold here (2 Sam 14:1-20; 20:14-22; 1 Kgs 3:16-28).

We shall call Dan 2, 4, and 5 examples of the "court wise man story." Variations in the pattern will be noted in the commentary on each chapter.

Daniel 2 is a complex chapter that introduces as a major theme the interpretation of dreams and emphasizes the wisdom theme by using a genre from Israel's worship, a hymn of thanksgiving (vv. 20-23). These elements will be discussed in the commentary on that chapter.

2. *Legends of Faithful Ones in Jeopardy.* This rather inadequate title enables us to group a small number of stories that show important similarities and to distinguish them from related stories of persecution or disgrace. They have sometimes been called martyr legends, but they are not, for the protagonists are saved from martyrdom. When they are compared with folktales concerning the disgrace and rehabilitation of a court figure, it is noticeable that only the Jewish stories make religion an issue. The stories in Dan 1, 3, and 6 may be called legends, following the now standard form-critical definition (a narrative primarily concerned with the wonderful and aimed at edification), because each is resolved by a miracle—obviously in the last two chapters, and it will be argued that chapter 1 is a miracle story as well. The term "jeopardy" has been chosen because in each case the hero's insistence on adhering to an essential aspect of the Jewish faith leads to a threat that is always overcome. The most useful parallels to the Daniel material appear to be Joseph's temptation by Potiphar's wife ("How then could I do this great wickedness, and sin against God?" [Gen 39:9]), and Susanna ("I choose not to do it; I will fall into your hands, rather than sin in the sight of the Lord" [v. 23]).

The pattern that appears in these passages is as follows: (1) pressure to disobey the law of God; (2) refusal, with one's insistence on remaining faithful to God explicitly stated; (3) judgment inflicted (in Dan 3 and 6, and Gen 39; pronounced but not inflicted in Susanna; avoided by means of a test in Dan 1); and (4) the protagonist delivered and vindication pronounced (by miracles in Daniel; by the introduction of the wisdom story in Gen 40–41; by Daniel's cleverness in Susanna).

The plot of the stories in Daniel may be summarized as follows: The lives of Jews are put into jeopardy because they insist on remaining faithful to the precepts of their religion, but the Jews persevere, and their God saves them, whereupon the king recognizes the superiority of the God of the Jews. It will be noted that the Joseph and Susanna stories vary slightly.

It will now be noted that a major theme runs through all six of the stories in Daniel. Both superior wisdom and the vindication of the faithful one lead to the same conclusion: all must acknowledge that the God whom the Jews serve is "God of gods and Lord of kings" (Dan 2:47).

The Genres in Daniel 7–12

Daniel speaks in the first person in chapters 7–12, and this is typical of accounts of visions, since only the visionary can know what has happened. Daniel's experiences have parallels in the vision-narratives found in the prophetic books. They introduce the experience with "I saw" and/or "he showed me" (for example, Isa 6:1; Ezek 1:4; 40:4; Zech 1:8; 3:3). What is seen is typically accompanied by dialogue, with God or an angel, in order that the meaning of the visual symbols may be made clear. Interpretation is necessary, for the visions are symbolic, rather than of things to be taken literally. The emotional and physical reaction of the seer to his experience may conclude the account (Isa 6:5; Ezek 1:28b; Dan 7:28; 8:27; 10:8-11, 15).

Descriptions of visions are relatively rare in the prophetic books (see also 1 Kgs 22), but they provide a clear point of contact between Old Testament prophecy and Daniel. The vision became a typical feature of apocalyptic literature, and two distinct types have been identified. One takes the seer on otherworldly journeys, something that does not appear at all in Daniel. The other is called the "historical apocalypse," since it focuses on explaining the course of earthly history, leading to its consummation. Daniel 7, 8, 9:24-27, and 11 are early examples of this type.

Jewish apocalyptic literature shows a great deal of individuality, and apocalyptic literature has been hard to describe as a genre because of that. Each work has its peculiarities, but there are enough similarities that distinguish a group of these books from earlier prophecy and other contemporary works; thus, there is fairly general agreement on which books should be called apocalypses. Daniel shares the following features with other apocalypses:

1. *Pseudonimity.* As noted above, the "Daniel" who recorded the visions seems to have lived in the second century, not the sixth, even though the book in its present form identifies the visionary who speaks in the first person in chapters 7–12 with the hero of chapters 1–6. All the apocalypses follow the same practice, iden-

tifying the author as someone from the distant past, except for Revelation, which claims to be by Christ's servant John (not necessarily the same as the apostle John).

2. *Use of symbolic visions.* Daniel and many other apocalypses use animal symbolism. Numbers and colors also require interpretation rather than being taken literally (for example, the white hair of the Ancient of Days in chapter 7).

3. *Evidence of a philosophy of history.* The "historical apocalypses" attempted to find meaning in history in various ways. Often it is divided into periods, as a way of showing order. Daniel 7 is an early example of this technique. The nearness of the consummation of history can then be demonstrated by showing that the readers are living in the next-to-last period.

4. *Hope in spite of pessimism.* Apocalyptic thought is essentially pessimistic regarding human potential for correcting the evils that prevail. Hope is offered solely on the basis of the conviction that divine intervention is near (note Dan 2:45; 8:25).

5. *An air of secrecy.* The aim of apocalyptic literature is to reveal mysteries (of the meaning of history, of the reason for evil on earth, of the end time, of heaven and hell). The intent is not to bewilder, but the atmosphere must remain mysterious somehow. So in chapter 11, where symbolism is not used, the Ptolemies and Seleucids, whose names the reader can supply from other sources, are simply called "king of the south" and "king of the north." The idea that the teachings of the book are to remain sealed up until the end of time (Dan 12:4, 9) also appears in other similar works.

Daniel differs from many other apocalypses in several respects:

1. The dualistic tendencies that led to speculation about the powers of evil, Satan, and the demons, are missing. Daniel remains close to the earlier Old Testament materials in this respect.

2. Speculation about heaven and hell is missing. Here also, Daniel is in continuity with the Old Testament in focusing on human destiny on earth.

3. Daniel differs from other apocalyptic literature and also from the eschatology of the prophetic books in its omission of descriptions of what the future ideal kingdom on earth will be like (contrast, for example, Isa 65:17-25; Ezek 36:24-38; and Zech 7–8).

This book goes no further than to say, "Their kingdom shall be an everlasting kingdom, and all dominions shall serve and obey them" (7:27b), and to promise resurrection in 12:2-3.

It seems likely that most of the authors of apocalyptic literature did have visionary experiences that led them to choose that genre to express their messages, although it may well be that some were imitators. Visions are a solitary event, and no one but the visionary can know what actually happened, or whether anything happened. The apocalyptic books are works of learning, not just the ramblings of people who have had bizarre experiences. They tend to be carefully structured and clearly intend to be understood in spite of the air of mystery that is typical. Although no one can be sure of this, it seems likely that the vision-accounts that did begin with an actual paranormal experience have been thought through by the seer and then written in such a way as to make sure that the message the seer discerned in the vision would be clear to the reader. We must allow for another possibility, as well. If "visions" had simply become a standard literary type, then some authors, without any intent to deceive, may have created them using the familiar symbolism, knowing this was what their readers would expect. Since only the authors could know whether their work originated with their imagination or with a real vision, speculation on that subject will be of no avail.

Use of Earlier Traditions

The book makes a creative use of a wide range of traditions. The familiar pattern of the court wise man story has been turned into an effective way of demonstrating the superiority of the God of a group of exiles even to the king of the greatest empire on earth. Within that pattern, the technique of dream interpretation, a very important means of learning the will of the gods in the ancient Near East (but of minor significance in the Old Testament), is used for the same purpose in chapters 2 and 4 (Oppenheim 1956, 179-373).

A mythological theme dominates the dream in chapter 4. Nebuchadnezzar sees the cosmic tree (used also in Ezek 31), which appears not only in Mesopotamian and Egyptian mythology but also in other cultures around the world. As in Ezekiel, however, the tree that should represent the stability of the cosmos is cut down. In both cases the king has first been assimilated to the world-tree, glorifying him, but its felling represents divine judgment of the king's *hybris*.

The references to beasts coming up out of the sea in chapter 7 have been compared with the depiction of the sea as a threatening monster in the Ugaritic myths and in the Babylonian creation epic, *Enuma Elish*. It has also been suggested that their composite character (for example, like a leopard with four wings on its back and having four heads, Dan 7:6) is due to the author's knowledge of another Mesopotamian tradition, that of taking births of animals with unnatural features to be omens that needed to be interpreted (Porter 1983).

Angels (literally, "messengers") appear from time to time in the Old Testament. They appear as interpreters of Zechariah's visions. Daniel represents a move toward the development of angelology that became prominent from the second century on, for angels are given names for the first time (Gabriel, 8:16; 9:21; Michael, 10:13, 21).

Traditional language of prayer, specifically the prayer of repentance, appears in 9:4-19. There are bits of poetry here and there in the book, all of it in praise of God. Daniel's hymn in 2:20-23 belongs to the wisdom tradition. The others are fragments that have been compared with the psalms of the kingship of Yahweh (e.g., Pss 92, 95–99), in that the extent and endurance of his dominion are the repeated subjects (4:3, 34-35; 6:26-27; 7:13-14, 23-27).

The author was clearly a learned person who could use for a new purpose themes and genres drawn not only from wisdom, prophecy, and worship in the Jewish world but also from the cultures in which he lived.

Style

There are so many echoes of other parts of the Old Testament in Daniel that his style has appropriately been called "anthological." We have seen some evidence of that in the preceding sections, but more can be added.

The language and themes of Deutero-Isaiah reappear a remarkable number of times in Daniel (Gammie 1981, 282-92). The hymns use some familiar expressions: "He knows what is in the darkness, and light dwells with him" (2:22; cf. Isa 45:7); "All the inhabitants of the earth are accounted as nothing" (4:35; cf. Isa 40:17). Isaiah 40–55 delights in making fun of idol worship (44: 9-20; 46:1-7), and idolatry is scorned in Dan 3 and 5. Several scholars have noticed less obvious parallels with the Servant Songs (Isa 42:1-4; 49:1-6; 50:4-9; 52:13–53:12). Daniel and his friends are called God's servants (3:26; 6:21), the spirit rests upon Daniel (4:8, 9, 18; 5:11; Isa 42:1), and the same root for wisdom *(śkl)* is used of God's gift to Daniel (1:7) and to the servant (Isa 52:13). It is thought that the promise of resurrection in Dan 12:2-3 represents the earliest interpretation of the promise concerning the servant in Isa 53.

The term *pĕšar,* interpretation, is used nineteen times in chapters 2, 4, and 5 to refer to Daniel's explanation of Nebuchadnezzar's dreams and the handwriting on the wall. By the time the vision accounts were written, the need for interpretation of the Scriptures was being felt, as Dan 9 reveals. He puzzles over what appears to be an unfulfilled prophecy in Jer 25:12 (cf. Jer 29:10), that after seventy years of desolation Jerusalem will be restored. After Daniel's prayer of repentance for his people's sins, Gabriel then explains that seventy really means seventy weeks of years (that is, four hundred ninety). Daniel thus contains an early example of a type of interpretation of Scripture that is now well represented in the documents from Qumran. The assumption is that the Old Testament texts must be speaking of one's own present and immediate future; in the Dead Sea Scrolls scripture is quoted, then its explanation is introduced with the Hebrew cognate to the word used in the Aramaic of Daniel, *pišrô,* "its interpretation (is)."

The style of the Aramaic stories differs noticeably from the typical way stories are told in the Hebrew Bible. Hebrew narrative style is usually very concise, with little or no description, and focusing on speech and action. On the rare occasions when an author begins to pile up words the reader is thus made aware:

"Now this is important—pay attention!" (For classic examples, note Gen 22:2, 9-10.) In contrast, the Aramaic stories seem very wordy. For example, people do not just "say," they always "answer and say." Part of that seems to be that Aramaic had become an international language, used as a second language by people all over the Persian empire; as a result, convenience rather than elegance influenced its grammar and syntax. But our author has also made deliberate choices to use a lot of repetition for effect. So we encounter not just "wise men" or "counselors," but "magicians, the enchanters, the sorcerers, and the Chaldeans" (2:2), and not once but several times. Nebuchadnezzar does not assemble his "officials," but the "satraps, the prefects, and the governors, the counselors, the treasurers, the justices, the magistrates, and all the officials of the provinces" (3:2), and the same list is repeated immediately in the next sentence. The list of musical instruments is provided four times within twelve verses. The modern reader is likely to become impatient with such a leisurely style, but it clearly was done deliberately; and when the stories are read with an effort to appreciate what the author is up to, it can be seen (or rather heard) that a unique effect is produced that would be lost if the stories were efficiently edited.

Structure

There is a chronological pattern that is somewhat unexpected but clearly represents an intentional effort to bind together the stories and the visions. The stories move chronologically from the reign of Nebuchadnezzar in chapters 1–4 through the reigns of Belshazzar (chap. 5), Darius the Mede (chap. 6), to Cyrus (6:28). We are already alerted in 1:21 that the first year of Cyrus will be the endpoint; so the six chapters are held together in this way. The visions are dated, taking us back to the first year of Belshazzar (7:1), his third year (8:1), the first year of Darius (9:1), and the third year of Cyrus (chap. 10).

As the book progresses, interest in the sequence of empires changes somewhat. In chapters 2 and 7 there are four, beginning with Babylon. Chapter 8 ignores Babylon and begins with the Medes and Persians. Chapters 7 and 8 each introduce the hellenistic period briefly in order to focus on Antiochus IV. This pattern of successive empires is alluded to in chapter 11, with brief references to Persia, then to Alexander and the division of his empire (vv. 2-4). The structure of the earlier chapters is dropped from this point on in favor of a detailed recital of the rule of the Ptolemies and Seleucids over Judea.

Another pattern has been detected within the Aramaic parts, supporting the idea that they may have existed as a book before the Hebrew parts were written. There is evidence of a chiastic structure. Chapters 2 and 7 bracket the section with their focus on the four empires. Inside that envelope are the two stories of death-threats to the three friends and Daniel (chaps. 3 and 6). In the center are two stories of the judgment of kings (chaps. 4 and 5; Lenglet 1972, 169-90).

DANIEL AS A WORK OF THEOLOGY

Although the book has two distinct parts that may have origi-nated in different times and places, the exilic setting that is pro-vided for the whole book is appropriate for its message. The book aims to strengthen and encourage Jews who are under pressure to compromise or abandon their religion. The issue was not identical for those in exile in Babylonia and for those in Judea at the time of Antiochus IV. Most of the former felt pressure to conform because they were the minority group who had lost the war and were living among the victors whose culture was rich and appar-ently superior. The temptation would be to admit the majority must be right and to take advantage of the opportunities that might be available to those who would assimilate. For Judeans in the 160s, however, the issue was life or death. It was a time when suffering martyrdom for one's faith became a reality (2 Macc 6–7).

There was a single issue that had to be decided for both groups, however, and the answer this book gives appears consistently in every chapter. There was once a radio program whose title sums up the crucial question the book of Daniel (and apocalyptic liter-ature as a whole) answers as forcefully as possible—"Who's in Charge Here?"

The stories all take place in the court of a great king, and there is no question that he and his gods claim to be in charge. His empire dominates the world. But when some Jews refuse to accept his claim to absolute power over them, they are sentenced, then vindicated, and the emperor himself must admit they are right (chaps. 1, 3, and 6). When he is baffled by a mysterious omen, only a Jew finds the resources to explain it, and the emperor confesses the remarkable power of the God of the Jews (chaps. 2, 4, and 5).

In the first vision, Daniel sees the heavenly court itself pass judgment on the arch-tyrant and then dares to announce, at a time when there seems to be no hope of human resistance, that soon a greater power will intervene and the tyrant will be no more. It is the claim for the absolute sovereignty of the God of Israel over all earthly powers (celebrated in the hymnic fragments noted above) that runs through the book as its major theme.

The intended effect on the readers is thus equally clear: the circumstances surrounding you may challenge everything you believe—either subtly or with deadly force. But there is a truth about reality that cannot be seen, and it has been revealed to Daniel. Someone else is in charge, and we know who it is. Your task is to believe and remain faithful, and you may live to see vindication.

I deliberately worded the last claim "you may live to see vindication," because the stories, with their happy endings, seem at first reading to be completely unrealistic. Faithfulness does not always lead to a nice promotion, by any means, and so it is important to recognize that this book also knows what real life is like. The commentary will emphasize the importance for all the stories of the friends' rejoinder to Nebuchadnezzar: "If our God whom we serve is able to deliver us from the furnace of blazing fire and out of your hand, O king, let him deliver us. But if not, be it known to you, O king, that we will not serve your gods and we will not worship the golden statue that you have set up" (3:17-18). They believe God will save them, but they know God is free and may choose something else. That makes no difference; they will do what is right because it is right.

The visions were written when people were not being promoted because of their faithfulness, but were being tortured to death. The date of the final form of the book saves us from dismissing the stories as "Sunday school stuff," thinking we realists know better. The people to whom the visions were addressed knew better also; but even so, they found something in the stories they needed to hear.

Daniel is unusual for an Old Testament book in that it focuses on a few individuals as role models. Elsewhere the only hero in the Old Testament is God. We certainly should not take everything Jacob or David did as examples of the moral life. But Daniel and his friends are not depicted as thoroughly human, the way other Old Testament characters are. They have committed no sins that we know of and are clearly intended to be models of the way a good Jew should behave. Daniel's prayer of confession in chapter 9 is really an intercessory prayer on behalf of his people, another example of his righteousness. This prayer, with its references to Israel's history, reminds us of another distinctive feature of the rest of the book—its individualism. The other Babylonian exiles must be in the background somewhere; however, they are invisible. We know only of Daniel and his three friends, and nothing of their families, not to mention the community. This is a very different outlook from the rest of the Old Testament, but in addition to the focus on an individual as a role model, there may be another reason for it. The exile would have broken up families, and many people probably had to face the future more alone than had been customary for Israelites until then. In the second century, to accept suffering and death while under persecution was probably the most intensely personal decision one would ever be called upon to make. Thus, there may be some good reasons for the unusual individualism of most of this book.

If Antiochus IV Epiphanes was the arch-tyrant of the visions, as all the evidence indicates, and if the visions were recorded during the persecution, then the promises of his demise, accompanied by the establishment of an eternal kingdom of righteousness, create an ongoing problem for the reader. Antiochus did die soon, but the kingdom seems not yet to have come, and certainly not the resurrection promised in 12:2. The issue of unfulfilled prophecy appears to be a major defect of this and other apocalyptic works (and not only those books, for Jesus and Paul also claimed that the consummation was near). Can we avoid saying the book of Daniel was wrong in this respect, and if it was wrong, does not that raise a serious question about its value and its inspiration?

One response to that serious question has been to insist that since Daniel is Holy Scripture, it could not be mistaken; so some way must be found to justify projecting the unfulfilled parts into our own future. A few of those many attempts were sampled in the first section of this introduction, and their shortcomings are easy to see. If we are willing to make one allowance for an inspired author, then something may be claimed for the value of a book that did not get it all right.

The allowance is this: no human being knows anything about the future. We can plan for it, can speculate about it, can hope and fear, but it remains beyond our control, and "knowledge" is not an appropriate word to use of it. There is nothing like accurate, detailed prediction of the future in the prophetic books of the Old Testament, and the unique, amazing details of Dan 11 are best understood as not being prediction after all. Jesus admitted that even the Son does not know the time of the end, but only the Father (Matt 24:36); so it should be accepted that humanness involves a hidden future, and that applies even to what Scripture can tell us about it. Daniel was partly right. The death of the tyrant was in fact near, and that is what his first readers most need to know.

I offer here a personal approach to books such as Daniel that speak of the nearness of the end. I was writing a short book on Ezekiel, and had come to the Gog chapters (chaps. 38–39). Needing time to reflect on what to say about them, I picked up the new *National Geographic* and read an article about the Aleutian Islands. Someone was telling the author about the abominable weather in the islands and said, "It's not the end of the world, but you can see it from there." I thought, that was what it was like for the writers and readers of the apocalyptic books. For all they knew, the end was upon them; for the martyrs the end—of this life—did come. For others it was not the end after all, but they could see it from there, and what they needed was a word for those facing the end. Apocalyptic literature intended to offer such a word, and it was a word of hope. Those who suffer need to have one question answered above all, and that is "How long?" These books answered, "It will not be much longer; be faithful and endure." Certainly there were times when the suffering lasted too long, and yet those who believed and did survive did not decide Daniel and Revelation were really wrong after all. That must be because there is something in the books more important than the expectation that the end is near, and it is surely the answer to the first question: "Who's in charge here?" Readers then and throughout history have not found that history and their own experiences have falsified the answer these books give: it is the God of Israel.

COMMENTARY

DANIEL 1

The first story in the book of Daniel functions as an introduction to the stories in chapters 2–6, and also contains a few ties to the visions in the remainder of the book. It is more than an introduction, however, for it could stand alone, as it develops in its own way a major theme: the tension that confronted Jews in exile between opportunities to succeed and pressure to compromise one's faith.

Literary Analysis

Daniel 1 has not attracted as much attention as the other five stories in the extensive recent discussions of genre. There is general agreement that chapters 2, 4, and 5 share essentially the same genre, and that chapters 3 and 6 are examples of another genre (see the introduction). Most interpreters have not seen chapter 1 as a good parallel to chapters 3 and 6, since there is no death threat made obvious and no sensational miracle of deliverance. The introduction, however, grouped the three chapters under the category "Legends of Faithful Ones in Jeopardy," and further support for that will be offered here. Chapter 1, like the other two, tells of Jews who must decide whether to compromise what they believe to be an essential part of their religion. In each story they decide not to give in, although in chapter 1 the stand they take does not involve a direct challenge to the king. The only explicit threat mentioned in chapter 1 is to the palace master (v. 10), but any reader may wonder what the results would have been for the young Jews if Nebuchadnezzar had found them to be in poor physical condition and on inquiry had learned that they had refused his hospitality. Danger seems logically to be implied, although not emphasized as it is in chapters 3 and 6. In the reading that follows, it will be emphasized that a miracle is present, when the youths prove to be healthiest of all, in spite of their scanty diet, even though the miracle is not described as explicitly as it is in the other two chapters. In comparing the three chapters, movement toward heightened danger may be seen: from an implied threat (chap. 1) to death for the three friends who otherwise appear only incidentally (chap. 3) to death for the hero of the book (chap. 6).

Whether chapter 1 was written later than the other stories and added as an introduction to the book, as some have suggested (thus offering an explanation why it is in Hebrew and the others in Aramaic), cannot be determined with certainty from the evidence available to us. That it does serve well as an introduction is clear, however. Most of the book shows no interest in the classic history of Israel, but verses 1-2 connect Daniel and his friends with that history. They also point to Daniel's prayer in chapter 9, in which the fall of Jerusalem plays a central role. The sacred vessels that Nebuchadnezzar captured reappear at Belshazzar's feast (5:2-3).

Although this is not a "court wise man story," details that make a connection with chapters 2, 4, and 5 are included. Wisdom, which is the gift of God, is bestowed on the four youths (1:10), and Daniel's ability to interpret visions and dreams anticipates what is to come. Even a major-plot element of the court wise man story is intimated: Already the king finds the Jews to be ten times wiser than all the magicians and enchanters in his whole kingdom (v. 20). The last verse of the chapter provides an envelope for the whole period during which the book of Daniel is set, since it begins with Nebuchadnezzar and ends with the reign of Cyrus (cf. 6:28; 10:1).

Exegetical Analysis

The "Historical Introduction" (1:1-2)

The first verse of the book introduces the first historical question. The reference to Nebuchadnezzar's capture of "vessels of the house of God" fits the events of 597 and 587 (2 Kgs 24:13; 25:14-

15) rather than the date provided in Dan 1:1. The date and events described do not easily correspond with the information in 2 Kings, 2 Chronicles, or Jeremiah, and seem to be contradicted by the Babylonian Chronicle. In 605 BC Nabopolassar, king of Babylonia, died shortly after his son Nebuchadnezzar had won a major victory against the Egyptian army at Carchemish. Jeremiah 46:2 refers explicitly to that victory and dates it in the fourth year of Jehoiakim; this event must have occurred before the attack on Jerusalem of which Dan 1:1-2 speaks, but the book of Daniel says that happened in Jehoiakim's third year. Jeremiah 25:1 calls Jehoiakim's fourth year the first year of Nebuchadnezzar, and 25:9 offers no clue that Nebuchadnezzar had attacked Jerusalem before this. In Jer 36:9, the fifth year of Jehoiakim, Nebuchadnezzar's coming is still in the future. Efforts to harmonize Daniel and Jeremiah claim that one used a calendar beginning in the spring, and the other a calendar beginning in the fall. This could account for Jer 25:1 and 46:2, but leaves 36:9 unexplained. Second Kings 24:1-2 speaks of a three-year period when Jehoiakim accepted a vassal status then rebelled, leading to the attack on Jerusalem that led to the first exile. No date is given, but this must have come at the end of his eleven-year reign, and so does not correspond with Dan 1. Second Chronicles 36:5-8 offers no date either, but appears to describe the events of 597. Thus, there is no hint in Scripture of an attack on Jerusalem in the third or fourth year of Jehoiakim. The only evidence that can be appealed to by those who defend the historical accuracy of these verses comes from the Babylonian Chronicle, which says that after the death of Nabopolassar, Nebuchadnezzar "went back again to the Hatti-land" (the term used of Syria-Palestine), with "again" suggesting he had been there after the victory at Carchemish and might thus have laid siege to Jerusalem. No such campaign is mentioned in the previous year, however (Grayson 1975a, 100). Evaluating the evidence, the most one can say is that Dan 1:1-2 is not completely impossible; but there is nothing positive to support it anywhere, and the other texts suggest it speaks of an exile to Babylonia earlier than any event that really happened. Most commentators suggest the author misread the three years of servitude

of which 2 Kgs 24:1 speaks. Rabbinical scholars recognized the problem and interpreted Dan 1:1 as a reference to the third year of Jehoiakim's rebellion, not of his reign. The verses remain problematic, but their primary intention is to claim that what follows will contain lessons to be learned from an otherwise poorly documented but crucial period in Jewish history, the Babylonian exile.

The Opportunity (1:3-7)

After the brief reference to Nebuchadnezzar as conqueror, the succeeding verses display him as one who intends to do well by selected members of the Israelite royal family. Nebuchadnezzar's own texts indicate that he supplied rations for captives from throughout his empire, including King Jehoiachin and other Judeans, who are mentioned on several tablets (Pritchard 1955, 308). He made use of the skills of exiles in his building projects (see 2 Kgs 24:14, 16), so the Dan 1 story of his "equal-opportunity-employment" practices fits what is known of his policies from other sources. Although the misery that resulted from the fall of Jerusalem, and the exile is abundantly testified to elsewhere in the Old Testament (e.g., Ps 137; Lamentations; Ezek 4–24), it is not emphasized at all in the stories in Daniel. The sins of foreign kings are condemned regularly by the prophets (e.g., Isa 14; Ezek 28–29, 31–32), but Dan 1–6 emphasizes opportunity in the service of a foreign king and not the terrible losses that really did affect the exiles. Those losses certainly lie in the background, but Daniel leaves them there, and does not bring them to the foreground, as a liberation-theology reading may be tempted to do.

Unlike most Old Testament books, which focus strongly on the weakest members of society, the book of Daniel is about the upper classes—those with potential for making a good new life, even in an alien land. The peasants had been left behind in Judah (2 Kgs 24:14; 25:12). Those chosen for service in the royal bureaucracy were "without physical defect and handsome, versed in every branch of wisdom" (1:4). This is reminiscent of a qualification for priests to serve in the Jerusalem temple, since they had to be without physical defect, but that seems irrelevant here; from what follows, it seems more likely this alludes to qualifications for the perfect scribe, for the youths are to be taught "the literature and language of the Chaldeans," presumably the Akkadian language (see Sir 38:34b–39:11).

The king "naturalizes" them by giving them Babylonian names (v. 7). The names seem to have been considerably mangled in the forms in which they appear in the Hebrew text—perhaps deliberately, since they probably contained the names of pagan gods. Some interpreters wish to emphasize the power claim that is made when a person's name is changed, but the author of Daniel does not make an issue of that. In fact, Jews from this period on took names from other languages and cultures without any appearance of finding the names to be problematic (e.g., Zerubbabel, "seed of Babylon," Ezra 3:2; Mordecai, perhaps based on the name of the god Marduk; and many Greek names from the hellenistic period on).

The Issue (1:8-17)

There is no indication of uneasiness about being given foreign names, about serving the king who had conquered their land, or even about becoming experts in the lore of Babylon, which would inevitably be infused with the beliefs of the local religion. But Daniel has a problem with eating the food the king intends to provide them. For Christians this would seem to be a truly minor issue, so it needs to be considered carefully. Three explanations have been offered:

1. Josephus claimed that Daniel was practicing a type of asceticism, choosing to "live austerely" (*Antiquities of the Jews* 10.10.2, sec. 190-94), and later readers appealed to the text as a commendation of fasting. Asceticism is scarcely found anywhere else in the Old Testament, and if such an attitude did exist in Daniel, it does not explain his concern not to defile himself.

2. On first reading, one might think the extensive food laws in the Old Testament to be the most natural explanation of Daniel's problem. Several questions arise, however. Wine is never prohibited in the kosher food laws. The only other texts that show a similar concern for eating food prepared by foreigners are later than Old Testament law, but they are roughly contemporary with the final form of Daniel: Tob 1:10-11; Jdt 12:1-4; Jub 22:16;

1 Macc 1:62-63 (for earlier texts, note Ezek 4:13; Hos 9:3-4). Some interpreters appeal to the kosher rules as the explanation of Daniel's behavior, but others question whether there is adequate support for thinking that, even in the second century BC, eating food prepared by Gentiles would have been this much of an issue. However, the only explanation offered by the text is the somewhat unusual word meaning "defile" (*gāʾal* II), which supports the thought that Daniel's problem does have to do with the ritual regulations of the Jewish faith.

3. The most popular current reading is similar to that of Calvin's; namely that Daniel found acceptance of the king's food to be "tantamount to declaring complete political allegiance" (Fewell 1988, 40; see also Towner 1984, 25-26). This reading is more appealing to Christians, since it makes Daniel's decision a completely moral one, not associated with ritual scruples. But is there any indication in chapters 1–6 that Daniel did not give the king *political* allegiance? He and his friends served in high and responsible positions in the government (3:48-49; 6:1-3). This reading would appear to be an example of the temptation to make an ancient text read in such a way that it poses no problems for modern sensibilities. Collins's judgment seems best to fit the text: "Refusal of the king's food was not a refusal of political allegiance but a declaration of separate identity and an affirmation of the unconquered dignity of the exiles" (Collins 1993, 146). For comments on the meaning of the dietary issue for contemporary readers, see the theological and ethical analysis.

They drank only water, but we cannot know exactly what they ate. The word *zērōʿîm* (v. 12; *zērĕʿōnîm* in v. 16) appears only here. It is evidently related to the word for "seed," and so is normally taken to mean they ate only grain products. This is not to be understood as a story advocating natural foods, or a vegetarian diet as providing superior nutrition. Such would weaken the impact the author wished to make, since the point is made throughout the chapter that the active agent in all that happens to the exiles is the God of Israel (note vv. 2, 9, and 17). Daniel and his friends chose a poor diet for themselves because of their concern about defilement, and it was in spite of, not because of, what they ate that they proved to be healthier and wiser than any of the rest of the candidates for royal service. This is a miracle story, although without the sensational elements of chapters 3 and 6.

The Outcome (1:18-21)

These were talented young men from the beginning (v. 4). Was it because of their decision to remain faithful to a principle of their religion they believed to be beyond compromise that God rewarded them with even greater gifts (v. 17)? It is possible to read the story that way, but note that the author does not speak explicitly of the result of the training period as a reward. Each of these stories does put a challenge before the reader: do you have the courage to withstand severe pressure to give up essentials of your faith? Each of them thus speaks of human responsibility and decision making, and each has a happy ending. A major theme, however, is the sovereignty of the God of Israel, this God's superiority to every earthly power, and the evidence of that is in the superiority of the gifts God gives to those who remain faithful to him. Daniel 3 makes it clear that endings may not always be happy; so reward for human faithfulness is a subordinate theme to the emphases on the power and grace of God.

Theological and Ethical Analysis

The first chapter of Daniel introduces two major themes concerning life in exile that reappear in chapters 2–6. The stories speak optimistically of the possibility of success—even while living under a foreign ruler—and offer an exclusively theological reason for it. It is because of the superiority of the gifts the one true God offers those who serve him. With the emphasis on the superior wisdom of the young Jews at the end of chapter 1, we are introduced to the stories of "wisdom contests" that appear in chapters 2, 4, and 5. The other major theme, however, is the warning that life in an alien culture will inevitably bring challenges to surrender and to accept as true and right the beliefs and ways of that culture. At times these may even become life or death issues, as chapters 3 and 6 emphasize. In chapter 1 the danger seems less, but we have already been introduced to a role model who will take risks in order to remain faithful to what he believes is right.

When a person is surrounded by people who do not believe or live as that person does, identity becomes a major issue, as it did for the Jews in the Diaspora. Who is a Jew, now that there is no homeland, no native government, no religious center (the Temple), and even the native language is being replaced? The issue of identity for a few involves not only the question "Who are you?" but also "Whose are you?" The latter question goes back to the Exodus. Yahweh demanded of the pharaoh, "Let my people go"—*my* people—claiming that those slaves belonged to him, not to the king of Egypt. (Note Lev 25:42: "For they are my servants, whom I brought out of the land of Egypt.") One of the ways the book of Daniel can speak very directly to the contemporary reader is by way of this frequently asked question of identity. "Who am I?" is a frequently asked question. When put into the context of faith and transformed into "Whose am I?" it brings us near to the questions Daniel faced. (On whom do I depend, and to whom am I responsible? On whom can I depend?) More will be said about the happy endings of these stories later, but it should be noted that those who read these stories, from earliest times, knew as well as we do that life often does not work out that well, yet they did not thereby reject the message they insist on, that there is a God who is worthy of our complete commitment.

It remains difficult for many Christians to appreciate the issue of diet in Dan 1 as a true crisis, and this is likely to lead to different readings of the passage among Christians and Jews who still observe the kosher food laws. The difference in attitude was well expressed by a rabbi friend of mine who commented that the worst thing Jesus ever said was, "It is not what goes into the mouth that defiles a person, but it is what comes out of the mouth that defiles" (Matt 15:11). (Knowing something about New Testament criticism, and wanting to defend Jesus if he could, he added, "Maybe Jesus didn't really say that.") Diet for my friend, as for Daniel, was an essential part of what defines a person as a Jew, and he thus remained within the long tradition that identified one's Jewishness by obedience to the Torah. Only since the nineteenth century, with the relaxation of dedication to the ritual law on the part of many Jews, has the question "Who is a Jew?" become a serious issue.

These reflections suggest a way for Christians to appreciate the challenge of Dan 1. How does one answer the question "Who is a Christian?" In Christianity, what corresponds to the definitive function of the Torah in traditional Judaism? Surely most would agree that confessing Jesus as Lord and Savior is primary, but how much more does one add as essential, if one is to claim to be a Christian? Diet has seldom been a major issue in Christian history, but there has been and continues to be great disagreement over which points of doctrine are essential, and how much freedom one should have in making ethical decisions. (Roman Catholics and Seventh-day Adventists are two examples of Christians for whom questions of diet have been important.) In parts of the world where being a Christian involves great social pressure and even danger, what is essential to the faith, and what can legitimately be compromised are questions that daily remain on the surface. Where Christianity is tolerated or dominant, the questions raised by the stories in Daniel can easily be ignored; but these stories may raise the issue for every reader, asking, Is it really wise—even safe—not to be clear about one's identity, not to have accepted something definitive that tells us who we are and then guides us in knowing what we must do?

DANIEL 2

Chapter 2 is a fully developed example of the court wise man story; however, Nebuchadnezzar's dream concerning four world empires contains certain parallels to chapter 7. So chapter 2 also serves as an introduction to the rest of the book, linking stories with visions.

Literary Analysis

The court wise man story has been expanded here with some important elaborations. As noted in the introduction, the question that motivates these stories is "Who has true wisdom?" In this case, the specific question is who is wise enough to know what the king dreamed, as well as know what the dream meant. The triumphant answer is, only Daniel, and only because the God of Israel gave him that wisdom as a special gift. This is the distinctively Israelite form of the wisdom story.

The pattern is complete: a king is the central figure; he faces a serious dilemma; his counselors are unsuccessful, but an outsider demonstrates true wisdom by appearing with the solution. Elaborations appear early. The impossible request—telling the king what he dreamed (not just what the dream meant, as in the Joseph story)—is more ominous than usual because it is accompanied by a death threat if the sages fail. Daniel (the true wise man) cannot be present at first, for that is not how these stories go, but the threat must include him and his companions in order to increase the tension. This makes the story not flow as smoothly as it might, as the exegetical analysis will note.

The next major elaboration is the prayer for wisdom, followed by the hymn to the God of wisdom. The prayer and hymn are not normal parts of these stories, but they are necessary here in order to make the theological point—Daniel's success is the work of God whose power surpasses anything the Babylonian sages can acquire. Recounting the dream and interpreting it are essential parts of the wisdom story, but they are such striking features that they have tended to draw attention away from the basic plot and to raise a question about the point of the chapter as a whole. Is the wisdom plot just a framework? That is in fact the effect the dream has had on most interpreters.

Dreams and their interpretation do not play a prominent role in the Old Testament. The only significant parallel to Dan 2 and 4 is the story of Joseph's success as a dream interpreter in Gen 41. There was substantial dream-literature in Mesopotamia, however. Oppenheim's thorough study provides helpful background information for the Daniel stories. He distinguishes "message dreams," which are straightforward communications from a deity or an emissary (cf. the dreams of Nabonidus in Pritchard 1955, 310), from "symbolic dreams," which require interpretation. The latter always dealt with future events (Oppenheim 1956, 207), so Nebuchadnezzar would have expected Daniel to refer to his dream as "thoughts of what would be hereafter" (2:29). If the dream was not understood, it was potentially dangerous; but once its message was revealed, the dreamer would be satisfied (Oppenheim 1956, 218-19). This would seem to account for Nebuchadnezzar's favorable treatment of Daniel, even though he has been told of the destruction of the statue, including the head of gold, which represented himself. Mesopotamian interpreters used several methods, sometimes simple intuition, often consultation of dream-books which explained various omens. They might also appeal, in various ways, to the deity who had sent the dream (Oppenheim 1956, 221; Lawson 1997, 61-76). Daniel's appeal to divine revelation is thus in line with Mesopotamian tradition. Note that the sages admit that "no one can reveal it to the king except the gods, whose dwelling is not with mortals" (2:11). But in this case the sages do not claim access to the gods.

Contemporary interpreters thus make a distinction between the proverbial wisdom known from the rest of the Old Testament and further developed in Wisdom of Solomon and Sirach, and "mantic" wisdom, which involves interpretation of dreams and omens. The latter is well known from Mesopotamian literature and thus would appear to be part of the authentic Mesopotamian background of the Daniel stories. In two ways this author associates mantic wisdom with the wisdom based on experience and observation. It is introduced into the familiar court wise man story, which more often attributes success to the intelligence and cleverness of the sage. And the hymn to the God of wisdom uses a series of synonyms ("wisdom," "knowledge," and "understanding") as in Prov 1:2-4, and has parallels with other wisdom poems such as Job 12:13-25; 28:23-27. At this time, the term "wisdom" refers both to what we would call "reason" and what we would call "revelation."

The hymn in verses 20-23 belongs to the genre "psalm of thanksgiving," beginning with praise of God, as the hymns in the Psalter do, but moving specifically to thanking God for responding to the author's request (cf. Pss 92, 116). Some commentators have claimed the poetry interrupts the course of the story and must have been a later addition, but most accept it as a meaningful part of the original work. At least three considerations support the conclusion that it is not an intrusion: If the main question of the court wise man story is "Who has true wisdom?" then the hymn, located as an introduction to the solution, is an impressive way of answering the question. Its contents allude to more than one element of the story—not only to God's revelation to Daniel, but also to the meaning of the dream ("deposes kings and sets up kings," v. 21) and to Nebuchadnezzar's reaction to the revelation (2:47).

In addition to the wisdom tradition, the chapter alludes to other ancient Near Eastern traditions that will be discussed in more detail in the exegetical analysis. Symbolic use of four metals appears as early as Hesiod's *Works and Days* (c. 730 BC), and sequences of four or more kingdoms appear in a variety of documents. Unfortunately, the dating of the materials in many of those documents is very uncertain, so one cannot with any certainty determine whether Daniel was using a pattern already well known in his time. Evidence from the more useful parallels will be discussed in the exegetical analysis.

Exegetical Analysis

The Dilemma and the Crisis for the Sages (2:1-12)

The date with which the chapter begins—the second year of Nebuchadnezzar—does not seem to correspond with the three-year period of training for the young men prescribed in 1:5. After training, they are introduced to the king (1:18), but in chapter 2 they already seem to be a part of the company of sages (2:13) and, in his second year, have already been promoted to high position (2:48-49). The problem has been variously explained, but it may be that the familiarity of the pattern of the court wise man story introduced some tensions with chapter 1 that could not be simply resolved. The pattern of the story requires Daniel to be an outsider; so in the second year of Nebuchadnezzar he would not yet be among the regular counselors, and he is not (vv. 1-12). The fact that he volunteers to Arioch and Arioch claims to have discovered him (vv. 24-25) also fits the pattern. However, other parts of the story correspond to chapter 1, which has Daniel and his friends already introduced to the king (1:18). They are included in the order to execute all the wise men of Babylon (2:12), and Daniel remarkably seems to have direct access to the king in verse 16. Efforts could be made to detect two stages in the composition of the story to account for these differences, but such dissections are always speculative; so this exegesis will allow the tensions to remain.

"His sleep left him" (v. 1) is one possible translation of the difficult Hebrew. We are left uncertain at this point whether he fell asleep again and forgot what he dreamed, or remained awake the rest of the night. It is clear that he was disturbed by it, and since all dreams were thought to have potentially threatening meaning, his immediate action to determine its meaning is understandable. The experts he calls in (denoted by, apparently, every technical term the author knows) are specialists in such matters, ready to serve. "Chaldean" was originally an ethnic term, not a designation of a specialist in divination, but it was regularly used the latter way by authors in the hellenistic period (Collins 1993, 137-38).

At verse 4 the language of the story changes from Hebrew to Aramaic, with the word "Aramaic" inserted to introduce the change. Although the theory to account for the two languages in the book (cited in the introduction) is a fairly convincing explanation of the book as a whole, for a story to begin in one language and shortly change to another remains without an adequate explanation.

The "impossible request" always creates the tension in a court wise man story, and it is put in a most extreme form here. To the counselors' reasonable request that the king tell them his dream, he replies that they must tell him what he dreamed, and if they cannot a dire fate awaits them. This is the always-dangerous, arbitrary power of the oriental potentate, and it also may be a reflection of the extent to which the dream has frightened him.

Opinions differ as to whether he had forgotten the dream or is withholding its contents as a test of how good the counselors' talents are. Most commentators now point out that he must have known enough of the dream to be able to recognize the sages' version, in order to be able to use it as a test.

The sages had access to a variety of techniques for the interpretation of dreams, as the Mesopotamian texts reveal, but to be asked to know what someone had dreamed was a new challenge. The lengthy appeal and refusal conclude with their admission that only the gods could do that (v. 11). They may have attributed their usual interpretations to divine revelation, but they had no experience with a request such as this. So the king, in "a violent rage," and probably in extreme anxiety, ordered them all executed.

Daniel and Arioch (2:13-16)

We are not told why Daniel and his companions are included with the condemned sages when Daniel and his friends had not been present at the initial scene, but the threat, of course, adds to the tension in the story and gives it something in common with chapters 3 and 6. Although Arioch has been instructed to execute the Jews, he plays a role of intermediary similar to that of the palace master in chapter 1. Daniel's ability to reason with these men is explained in 1:9 as a gift of God, and that is to be assumed here also. Daniel's apparent direct access to the king in verse 16 might be explained as another divine gift, but it seems to conflict with verse 25, where Arioch introduces him as his own discovery. Another surprise at this point in the story is the time that is apparently allotted to Daniel, unlike the other sages, without even mentioning the difference (note the abrupt move from v. 16 to v. 17). Unless the text has been disrupted at this point, presumably this is also to be taken as evidence of divine favor.

Daniel Appeals to God (2:17-23)

Daniel's companions appear in a subsidiary role in chapters 1 and 2 and are the central characters in chapter 3, after which they are not mentioned again. They face the same jeopardy as Daniel in the first two chapters and participate with him here in prayer for an inspired solution to the problem. Note that the hymn concludes with "for you have revealed to us" (v. 23). Daniel remains the speaker throughout, however, and he is said to have been the recipient of a "vision of the night" (v. 19; cf. 1:17; 7:1).

As noted in the literary analysis, the hymn is an example of a psalm of thanksgiving, with much of its content drawn from vocabulary and themes of the wisdom literature. It is an appropriate addition to a story whose theme is "Who has true wisdom?" and its poetic form makes an impressive way to mark the turning point in the story. In the introduction, Israel's God is referred to as "God of heaven," a title widely used during the Persian period. (It may be noted that the divine name "Yahweh" is used in Daniel only in chapter 9.) In addition to wisdom themes in the hymn, the hymn also clarified where power really lies, in contrast to the claims of Nebuchadnezzar (4:30) and the archtyrant (8:23-25; cf. changing the times and seasons in 2:21 and 7:25).

Daniel Explains the Source of His Wisdom (2:24-30)

Readers have been enlightened by the hymn; now the king must know why only Daniel can answer the impossible request. Proper protocol is followed this time. Arioch introduces Daniel to the king and assumes credit for finding him. Daniel is not identified as one of the sages, so the traditional wisdom plot (in which he should be an outsider) is maintained at this point, even though it conflicts with earlier elements of the story, for we are reminded he already has a Babylonian name, Belteshazzar.

What Nebuchadnezzar is really intended to learn from this experience (since the destruction of the statue will not affect him personally) is spelled out at some length in verses 27-30. There is a power (named only as "God of heaven") inaccessible to the great king except as that God has chosen to reveal himself through Daniel. We learn now that Nebuchadnezzar's dream concerns the future ("what will happen at the end of days," v. 28), but the studies of symbolic dreams noted above remind us that such dreams were always assumed to deal with the future (Oppenheim 1956, 207).

COMMENTARY

Daniel Reveals the Dream (2:31-35)

The appearance of an enormous figure in the dream of a king can be found elsewhere in ancient Near Eastern dream-narratives. In a Sumerian text, king Gudea reports seeing "in the dream, the first man—like the heaven was his surpassing (size), like the earth was his surpassing (size)" (Oppenheim 1956, 245). No parallel to the composite figure Nebuchadnezzar saw has been found, however. The symbolic use of the four metals—gold, silver, bronze, and iron—has been found in Greek, Latin, and Zoroastrian texts, and they sometimes represent empires. So the dream clearly makes use of themes that were "in the air" at the time. Efforts to find exact parallels in the other literature have not been successful, however (Collins 1993, 162-70). The feet of the image are a strange composite; partly of iron and partly of ceramic, not simply "clay," as in many translations (the Aramaic word is always used of fired clay objects; Montgomery 1927, 167; Kelso 1948, 6-7).

The dream becomes more unreal with the appearance of a stone "cut out, not by human hands" (from a mountain, we learn from v. 45), which moves by some unnamed force so as to strike the image on its feet. Not only are the feet shattered, and not only is the composite statue broken, as might happen in real life, but all the metals are pulverized and the wind blows them away. Finally, the stone grows until it has filled the whole earth. Stone is often used as a symbol of strength, and numerous such metaphors can be found in Scripture, but nowhere else does a stone behave like this one; so it is perhaps best not to make much of the rather distant parallels.

Daniel Interprets the Dream (2:36-45)

Daniel follows royal protocol by beginning the interpretation with words flattering the king, speaking of his rule over the whole earth in extravagant terms and affirming that the God of heaven has appointed him to rule. These are the words oriental monarchs typically used of themselves, but now a Jew seems to accept them as true, except for omitting the names of pagan gods. This is an example of the openness to life under foreign rulers that is typical

56

of the stories in Daniel, but it has a precedent in some of the prophetic books. Ezekiel, especially, speaks of the wisdom and wealth of the king of Tyre before pronouncing judgment because of his pride (28:1-23), then compares Pharaoh with the world-tree, the symbol of fertility and stability (chap. 31). The fact that government (i.e., the king) can produce security and prosperity for its people is thus acknowledged by these authors, even when they must declare the same governments to stand under judgment because of their excesses. The theme of judgment is not made explicit here, as it is in Dan 4 and 5, but it is implicit in the destruction of the image.

The identification of the empires Daniel describes was taken to be obvious for many centuries (except for Porphyry's dissenting view), but then became a matter of great controversy in the nineteenth and twentieth centuries. The head of gold is explicitly identified with Nebuchadnezzar, so all interpretations begin at the same point. One of the contemporary variant interpretations takes "you are the head" very literally and claims that only Nebuchadnezzar, not his empire, is meant. The remaining metals thus denote the kings of Babylonia who succeeded him. The dream can then be taken as a prophecy fulfilled with the fall of the Neo-Babylonian empire (Bickerman 1967, 62-68; Goldingay 1989, 51). There is little in the text that supports taking the metals as symbols of individual kings, however.

The prevailing reading through much of history (with exceptions noted in the introduction) assumed that the fourth kingdom must be Rome, the power of which would be well represented by iron. This reading made Alexander's kingdom the kingdom of bronze, "which shall rule over the whole earth" (v. 39); and that is appropriate. This leaves Persia for the second kingdom, and to explain why it is called "inferior" to Nebuchadnezzar's has required great ingenuity, for Persia was inferior in no respect.

The more natural reading, accepted by almost all commentators at present, is to take the second kingdom as the Medes ("inferior" inasmuch as it is of much less importance in Jewish history than Babylonia); the third as the Persians, well described as ruling the whole earth; and the fourth, crushing and shattering everything, as Alexander's. The division of his kingdom just after his death, and the diplomatic marriages that affected Jewish history (2:42-43; 11:6) are then easily to be seen as represented by the mixture of iron and ceramic in the statue's feet. The Roman theory has found it necessary to struggle to find historical references in this symbolism, which fits the hellenistic period much more clearly.

Why, then, did the church insist on the Roman theory? The answer is clear. The kingdom that shall never be destroyed (v. 44) should be the church, and the stone should represent Christ—so many argued, although the exact identities varied. Knowing how the dream *should* come out dictated the way the empires must be identified.

A stumbling block for complete acceptance of the sequence—Babylon, Medes, Persia, hellenistic kingdoms—has been the fact that there was no Median empire that intervened chronologically between the Neo-Babylonian and Persian kingdoms. Both internal and external reasons for the sequence can be found, however. The book explicitly speaks of kings of these four nations: Nebuchadnezzar and Belshazzar in Babylon, followed by Darius the Mede (5:30; chap. 6), and Cyrus the Persian (6:28). The defeat of the Medes and Persians by Alexander is the subject of chapter 8 (vv. 20-21), and the division between Ptolemies and Seleucids is detailed in chapter 11. Outside the Old Testament, the series Assyria, Medes, Persians, Greeks appears in Herodotus (1.95, 130) and in later texts (Collins 1993, 166-67; Swain 1940, 1-20). The Medes were a significant power in the Middle East for about a century, from the time of the demise of the Assyrian empire (late seventh century) until Cyrus moved the center of power to Persia (Caragounis 1993, 392-94). Even so, the fact that there was no chronological sequence of world empires—Babylonia, Medes, Persia—has troubled interpreters. The conclusion of the dream indicates that sequence was not an important part of it, however, for in the statue all parts are present at once and all are destroyed at once. The point of the dream, emphasized by the stone (a natural object in contrast to the metals), produced and acting supernaturally so as to make the image disappear completely, is the claim that the power of God will overcome all the power of human kingdoms.

Conclusion: Praise and Promotion (2:46-49)

Although Daniel's speech began with flattering words for Nebuchadnezzar (vv. 37-38), his explanation—that the dream meant the Babylonian kingdom would be supplanted, and the powers of all earthly kingdoms would eventually be destroyed—meant the king's dream truly was an ominous one. His reaction was altogether favorable, however. We are reminded of Oppenheim's observation that, in Mesopotamian texts, once a dream is explained its threatening aspects are felt to dissipate (Oppenheim 1956, 218-19). The recognition that Daniel does have access to true wisdom from his God, accompanied by appropriate rewards, also fits the pattern of the wisdom story. Not only is Daniel given a high position in the Babylonian bureaucracy, but his friends also are promoted, setting the stage for their trials in the next chapter.

The statement that Nebuchadnezzar bowed down to Daniel and made offerings to him as if he were divine has troubled commentators, since a good Jew should not have accepted acts of worship (note the reactions of Paul and Barnabas when identified with Hermes and Zeus, Acts 14:8-18). Jewish interpreters insisted that Daniel must have rejected Nebuchadnezzar's obeisance. Jerome's suggestion, that Nebuchadnezzar was really worshiping Daniel's God, is often quoted, but the author of the story may not have noticed this as a problem, the way later readers have done. He may have seen it as a fulfillment of texts such as Isa 45:14; 49:23; and 60:14 (Mastin 1973, 80-93).

Theological and Ethical Analysis

This is a message for people living in a relatively stable setting. There are no references to persecution (as in chaps. 7–12) and so there is no need for a promise of deliverance. The Jews live in exile, but there is no indication of a longing for, or promise of return to, the homeland. Although the king's power can be dangerous, he is not depicted as the enemy of God's people. The heroes of the story are very successful people.

Even so, the story is concerned with what it means to live as a minority within an alien culture, so it could be relevant to readers whether they lived in the Diaspora, or in Judea under the rule of Persians, Ptolemies, or the early Seleucids. The theological issue addressed by this story had been the same since the preexilic prophets dealt with it: having lost the wars with Assyria and Babylonia, and then finding themselves at the mercy of Persian and hellenistic kings, what did that say about their claims that Yahweh was creator of heaven and earth and sovereign over all of history? Was there any evidence that could be true? The prophetic insistence that Yahweh used Assyria and Babylonia to punish the sins of Israel and Judah had been accepted by the Jews after the fall of Jerusalem in 587 BC, but that did not explain their subsequent history. Partial restoration to their homeland had partly validated the prophetic promises that Yahweh had a better future in store for his people after the judgment, but the successes of Persians and Greeks left a great contrast between the existence of little groups of Jews in those immense empires, and the glorious pictures of the ideal future in the prophetic books.

Daniel will not repeat those promises, but instead takes a more vague concept found also in the Psalms—the kingdom of God—and says little more than to offer the reassurance that eventually the kingdom will be established on earth and will endure forever. His evidence that the God of the Jews does have some power, after all, is at this point the success of certain Jewish individuals in the pagan world. God's great power is not yet manifest at the scale of world history, but it can be seen in the gifts that enable those who believe in him to stand out. This helps to account for the individualistic nature of the stories, noted in the introduction. The introduction also noted that Daniel's use of the term "kingdom" has probably influenced the occurrence of the terms "kingdom of God" and "kingdom of heaven" in the New Testament (Wenham 1987, 132-34). Jesus, like Daniel, did not offer any extensive description of that kingdom. He spoke of its imminence, but as New Testament scholars have observed, the emphasis is not so much on *kingdom* as on *kingship*, the reign of God, and that is in continuity with Daniel.

Although there are obvious parallels between the composite statue and the four beasts that represent world empires in chapter 7, the static nature of the statue and the fact that it is all destroyed at once shows that the interpretations that emphasize the chapter as a prediction of future history may read a bit too much into it. The visions in chapters 7–12 are certainly intended to describe how history will unfold and what its consummation will be. This dream is similar, but its main point is in keeping with the usual conclusion of the court wise man stories. They always demonstrate the superiority of the outsider. Here it is not the outsider himself, but the outsider's God who is shown to be supreme, and in two ways. Only Daniel's God can reveal the dream and its meaning, and that ought to make one take seriously the meaning—that the same God intends one day to replace earthly kingdoms with a kingdom that will stand forever.

Daniel's double role, as wise man and visionary, illustrates a change in the understanding of wisdom in the Judaism of this period. The wisdom of Proverbs, Ecclesiastes, and Job is essentially rational. It can be acquired by learning from one's teachers and by developing the powers of observation, analysis, and classification. It was not "secular," since its content was strongly moral to the extent that wisdom was equated with righteousness, and God was the ultimate source of true wisdom. But except for one unusual passage in Job (4:12-16), the wise did not claim divine inspiration.

Daniel's wisdom, however, is associated with visions and dreams, and he does not offer good advice such as we find in Proverbs, or reflection on life's deepest problems (Job and Ecclesiastes). He is an interpreter of omens, and in chapter 9 interprets Scripture, with access to the truth by way of the divine Spirit. So Daniel's activities have been compared with the mantic wisdom of Babylonian texts, as noted above. They are in continuity with a development that appears in Sirach and Wisdom of Solomon, however, traced in Rylaarsdam's work *Revelation in Jewish Wisdom Literature* (Rylaarsdam 1946). "Where shall wisdom be found?" the book of Job asks, with a serious challenge to the adequacy of reason. The later wisdom books responded by equating wisdom with the Spirit. Subsuming both reason and revelation under the rubric of wisdom was thus a development taking place in various ways, and the wisdom texts from Qumran now provide additional evidence that these two apparently very different enterprises—inspired interpretation and reasoned analysis—were both called "wisdom" (Collins 1997, 265-81).

DANIEL 3

Daniel does not appear at all in this chapter. Some surmise the reason is that, since it is the only chapter in which Shadrach, Meshach, and Abednego play a significant role, it may be that this story originally existed independently and has been integrated into the book by adding the companions' names to chapters 1 and 2. The rabbis had a different explanation: Nebuchadnezzar was so impressed with Daniel's ability to interpret his dream that he would not consider consigning him to the furnace.

Literary Analysis

This is a classic example of the "legends of the faithful ones in jeopardy." It has been compared with the folktale pattern "disgrace and rehabilitation of a minister," and the ways it varies from that pattern will serve to introduce some of the unique features of the story: (1) The hero is in a state of prosperity. Eventually we learn this, for the story does not begin with the heroes. We hear of their status only when they are accused. (2) The hero is endangered. The Jewish forms of the story are unique in making a distinctive aspect of their religion the basis for the threat. (3) The hero is condemned to death or prison. Nebuchadnezzar meets with Shadrach, Meshach, and Abednego to determine whether the accusation is true and to give them a chance to comply with his decree, so they are not immediately condemned for their earlier refusal to pay homage to the image. This scene gives them the opportunity to state their position. They do not explain why (e.g., opposition to idolatry), but only offer their belief that their God will rescue them. The opportunity for testimony—so important in later martyr legends—is thus left undeveloped. (4) The hero is released, here because of a stupendous miracle. (5) His wisdom or merit is recognized and he is given a position of honor. Wisdom and honor appear at the conclusion of this chapter, as well as acknowledgement of the power of the God of the Jews.

The clearest parallel to this story is Daniel 6. The other parallels mentioned in the introduction differ somewhat from this story. In both Gen 39 and Susanna it is sexual desire and the refusal to commit adultery because of one's faithfulness to God that set the drama in motion. Neither protagonist is saved by a stupendous miracle. Susanna avoids the death penalty because of Daniel's cleverness, and Joseph goes to prison for a time, to be finally released, because of his ability to interpret dreams. A partial parallel appeared later, in the first martyr stories. In 2 Macc 6:18-31 the elderly scribe Eleazar was put on the rack because he refused to eat pork that had been sacrificed to a pagan god. The efforts of his torturers to induce him to apostatize gave him the opportunity to explain why he remained faithful. The first three parts of the folktale pattern are present, but instead of deliverance and promotion, he dies. Commendation of his merit does appear, however, in the words of the author. The story of the sufferings of the mother and her seven sons in 2 Macc 7 follows the same pattern.

A new genre of short story thus appears at this time, developing because of the problems created for Jews living within polytheistic cultures because of the uniqueness of their religion. Christians, inheriting the monotheism and anti-idolatrous theology of Judaism, would face the same issues and would take encouragement from similar stories of faithful witnesses.

The most prominent stylistic feature of this chapter is the repetition of lists and of key clauses. Three times we read the list of Nebuchadnezzar's officials (abbreviated the third time, v. 27). Four times the full list of musical instruments appears. The expression "the statue that King Nebuchadnezzar set up (or made)" occurs no fewer than ten times. The furnace is usually a "burning fiery furnace." "People, nations, and languages" occurs three times. The immediate effect of the lists and the sonorous expressions such as the last three expressions mentioned is to slow down the telling of the story, which certainly should be read aloud in order to appreciate that effect. Far from being comical, as a few recent authors have suggested, this piling up of words produces a stately effect, and it seems likely that the author chose the repetition because the sound corresponds to the meaning associated with all these terms. They all emphasize the power of Nebuchadnezzar (and the author keeps reminding us that Nebuchadnezzar is *the king*).

Nebuchadnezzar has an elaborate administrative system; at his command all those officials appear and fall down before the image that he has set up. The immense image is made of gold (we are reminded seven times), and the king has a full orchestra to initiate the cult associated with that image. These details reinforce the centrality of the king himself from beginning to end of the story. The heroes get only one speech (vv. 16-18). Verses 16-18 are the most important verses in the chapter, and that is perhaps emphasized by the fact that, except for their speech, Shadrach, Meshach, and Abednego are passive figures. Indeed, it is what they do not do that gets them into trouble. All the other characters are active (see theological and ethical analysis). One of the distinctions between the two genres in Dan 1–6 is that the heroes make long speeches in the wisdom stories (2:20-23, 27-45; 4:19*b*-27; 5:17-28), while they say very little in the jeopardy stories. Daniel speaks at the beginning in 1:12-13 and at the end in 6:21*b*-22. In each of chapters 1, 3, and 6, the brief speech makes clear the speaker's motivation and expresses the determination not to violate an essential precept of the Jewish religion, while the rest of the story describes how around the Jews the affairs of a mighty nation threaten to grind them up without regard to belief, dignity, or potential contributions they might make.

Exegetical Analysis

The Golden Image (3:1-7)

The story begins abruptly, as if the building of the image immediately followed the promotions of Daniel and his friends. The location of the image, in the plain of Dura, does not seem to be important, since nothing more is said of it. "Dura" ("wall/enclosure") is a word used in several Mesopotamian place names, so it cannot be located exactly. Golden statues (usually of wood or base metal covered with sheets of gold) are well documented as part of the ostentation of oriental kings. Herodotus (fifth century BC), for example, tells of a sitting figure of Zeus, all of gold, in the temple of Bel at Babylon (1.183). The dimensions of the image are very strange, however, about ninety feet tall and only nine feet wide, scarcely the dimensions of a human figure or any other upright creature. Commentators speculate as to what it might have represented, but we must remember that it existed only in the mind of this author, and may not correspond with anything in the ancient world. The question, then, is why the author chose such dimensions. We cannot answer that.

Of the seven offices that are named in verses 2 and 3, two are denoted by words of Akkadian origin and the rest are Persian, evidence supporting a fairly early origin for the story, but scarcely an accurate way to describe the administration of the Neo-Babylonian empire.

Having been told in verse 1 that king Nebuchadnezzar made the image, we are then reminded five times in the first seven verses that it is the statue that *he* had set up. We are not told what it represented; so opinions differ as to whether it was his image or that of a god. The accusation against Shadrach, Meshach, and Abednego—that they do not worship Nebuchadnezzar's gods (vv. 12, 14, 18, 28)—supports the latter. But when we are told ten times that this is *his* work, it seems evident that this is the only reason for the statue's importance. As already noted in the previous section, royal power dominates the story from beginning to end.

On command, all the ranks of bureaucrats assemble for the dedication of the image. Whether this involved officials only, or included the general populace (note "peoples, nations, and languages" in vv. 4 and 7), it seems clear as the story continues that the issue does not involve the Jewish population as a whole, but only Shadrach, Meshach, and Abednego, because they are officials whose loyalty to Nebuchadnezzar became suspect.

The "herald" who begins the ceremony is designated by the Aramaic word that may be derived from the Greek word *kērux*. Lists of musical instruments used in worship appear in other ancient Near Eastern texts, including Ps 150 (although the list in the psalm is entirely different). Three of these instruments have Greek names: *qytrs* (from *kitharis*), *psntryn* (from *psaltērion*), and *swmpnyh* (from *symphōnia*). Although there was some commerce between Greece and Mesopotamia as early as the Neo-Babylonian period, so that Greek words might have been known there, this cluster of words is much more likely to have been understandable after the extensive hellenization of the Middle East had begun (third century on). The instruments cannot be identified exactly, so translations will vary considerably.

The whole assembly was to bow down before the image, and the same verb is used that had been used of Nebuchadnezzar's obeisance before Daniel in 2:46. This was a most serious affair—the punishment for failure to bow down would be death by fire—but we are never told explicitly why the punishment was so severe. Extreme punishments for a great variety of crimes were part of life in the ancient Near East, but seldom involved burning (Jer 29:10 is one example). The Assyrian kings recorded gruesome penalties imposed on all who challenged their authority, and throughout this chapter the emphasis on the power of Nebuchadnezzar suggests that this ceremony was a kind of loyalty oath imposed on his officials. To refuse would imply treason, and treason is always subject to the death penalty.

The Accusation (3:8-12)

Certain Chaldeans noticed that three members of that group did not bow down, and took it upon themselves to report that traitorous behavior to the king. The three are identified as Jews, suggesting some ethnic rivalry; but since Judaism itself is not made an issue, it seems likely that "Chaldean" is used here, as in 2:2, to designate a certain specialty of divination, and that the rivalry was professional. The author wants us to know the accusers' motives were not altogether pure, for the "denounce" of the New Revised Standard Version is literally "ate their pieces (of flesh)." Compare the English idiom "backbiting." Nebuchadnezzar is reminded first of his decree concerning the image, then that these are officials he has appointed (cf. 2:49), thus owing loyalty to him.

The accusation is threefold, concluding with disrespect of the image and adding refusal to serve Nebuchadnezzar's gods, suggesting the image did represent a deity (v. 12). The accusation begins with the issue that motivates Nebuchadnezzar throughout the whole story: "These pay no heed to you" (with a remarkable play on the words used of issuing the decree in v. 10, evident only in Aramaic). The accusers can be sure Nebuchadnezzar will react to that.

Opportunity and Refusal (3:13-18)

In spite of his furious reaction, the king does not punish the three Jews for their obstinacy immediately, but gives them another chance to show their loyalty. He asks them if the accusation is true, and, without waiting for an answer, warns them that when the ceremony is repeated, if they do not bow down they will be thrown into the fiery furnace. Then comes another of the clear indications that absolute royal power is the issue that dominates the chapter: "and who is the god that will deliver you out of my hands?" (v. 15).

The king's two conditional sentences are now echoed by two conditional sentences from the three Jews:

If you are ready . . . But if you do not worship . . . (v. 15).
If our God . . . is able . . . But if not, . . . we will not serve . . . (vv. 17, 18).

The syntax of the first part of the answer is a bit unusual, but it has been meaning rather than syntax that has led to a variety of translations. The most natural reading of the Aramaic is represented by the New Revised Standard Version: "If our God whom we serve is able to deliver us. . . ." This suggests some uncertainty in the minds of the Jews, however, and readers from early times have found that unacceptable. The Old Greek and the Septuagint make it a bold affirmation: "There is a God in heaven," and "for there is a God, whom we worship, capable . . . " In the Vulgate the introductory particle *hēn* has been taken to be the Hebrew *hinnēh* "behold" rather than the Aramaic "if." The King James Version and the Revised Standard Version offered a vague rendering, "If it be so. . . . " Even two contemporary translations have been unwilling to let their readers face the uncertainty in the sentence and have "corrected" the Aramaic: "If we are thrown into the blazing furnace, the God we serve is able to save us from it (NIV); "The God we worship can save us" (CEV). Commentators all agree that the if-clause must be preserved, but point out that it may not be God's *ability* to save as much as God's *intent* that the Jews are unsure of.

Were they being depicted as superheroes absolutely sure of themselves and their God, as every reader likes to think, or does verse 17 make them very normal people who would surely have been trembling at the prospect of death by fire? Under those circumstances an ordinary person might not feel as certain as usual about what could really be believed. Real life appears without question in the next sentence, "But if not . . . ," and perhaps the author intended to introduce the seriousness of the challenge to faith in verse 17, making the heroes more like the rest of us than they would otherwise have seemed to be. As even Jesus went into Gethsemane "grieved and agitated" (Matt 26:37), so these men may have approached the furnace fearfully, and if so, their next statement is all the more impressive.

No questions have been raised about the meaning of verse 18. They believe (or hope) that God will deliver them, even from a burning, fiery furnace, but they know God is free and that neither they nor anyone else can put any constraints on the divine will. The first of the martyr legends, probably written not long after this, has to deal with the reality of death under torture, with never a miraculous rescue. The author of this story knows one cannot count on rescue. The position taken by the heroes thus represents the highest kind of motive: doing the right thing only because it is right.

The Furnace (3:19-23)

In chapters 2 and 3 Nebuchadnezzar falls into rages easily. In this chapter (vv. 13 and 19), even his anger may reinforce the emphasis on his absolute power, for what could be more terrifying than the rage of someone who could do to a person anything he wished? He does not indulge in torture, however, but takes the rather ineffectual course of having the furnace heated seven times hotter than was customary—not that they had gauges; the number is used for effect. How that would have made the Jews' fate worse is not explained; the order seems to reveal an irrational reaction to this challenge to his authority. In fact, it rebounds in that some of his soldiers are killed (v. 22). Some commentators are troubled by the injustice of it, for the guilty ones, the Chaldeans, go free, while soldiers who are just doing their duty are killed. Here is another reflection of how it is in real life, however.

Discussions of the probable shape of the furnace may be found in other commentaries, but they are hypothetical and of no great importance for understanding the text. All we need to know is that there was an open door through which the king expected to see the immolation of these former officials who had dared to challenge him.

Deliverance and Recognition (3:24-30)

Nebuchadnezzar remains the central character in the story, in that the description of the miracle is put into his mouth. Instead of seeing three men lying bound in the midst of the flames, he sees four, unbound, walking about in the furnace. The fourth has the appearance, he says, of a "son of gods (Aramaic)," that is, a divine being of some sort. What such a being would have looked like to Nebuchadnezzar (or to the author) we can only guess. A little later (v. 28) he speaks of an angel. Angels are not described in the Old Testament except to indicate that they have a humanlike form. (For discussion of the role of angels in Daniel's visions, see chap. 10.)

"Son of gods" was close enough to "Son of God" for Christian interpreters from early times to find Christ there in the furnace with the three Jews. Already, Hippolytus assumed that to be true, then wondered how Nebuchadnezzar, a pagan, could have recognized him. But "son of God" (or in Nebuchadnezzar's speech, "gods") was a common Semitic idiom used to denote heavenly beings, as in Gen 6:2; Pss 29:1; 82:1, 6, or the Judean king as an adopted son (Ps 2:7). We hear nothing more of the mysterious figure except Nebuchadnezzar's conclusion that he had been sent by the God of the Jews to deliver his faithful ones.

Nebuchadnezzar orders Shadrach, Meshach, and Abednego to come out of the furnace, and they do, silently. The testimony that a stupendous miracle has occurred comes from the other officials, who can find no evidence that the Jews have even been in the fire (v. 27). Only Nebuchadnezzar speaks, however. He calls the three "servants of the Most High God" (v. 26), but this is scarcely evidence of a conversion. "Most High God" was another common Semitic term found in extrabiblical Aramaic (Fitzmyer 1995, 37-38), and put into the mouth of Melchizedek, a Gentile king, in Gen 14:19-20. Here it is not to be taken as a monotheistic term. Nebuchadnezzar praises Shadrach, Meshach, and Abednego now for disobeying him, trusting in their God and giving their bodies rather than serving or worshiping any god but their own (v. 28). The language of martyrdom, "giving their bodies," already appears.

The king has been taken aback momentarily. What he saw in the furnace had amazed or even frightened him (v. 24), and he must acknowledge the power of the God of these Jews; but he recovers quickly. After his "blessing" (v. 28), he immediately reasserts his authority, with a new decree: anyone who insults the God of Shadrach, Meshach, and Abednego shall be subjected to a horrible death (v. 29). And he not only keeps the three Jews in his service, but promotes them, as always happens in legends of this type. The legitimacy of the Jewish religion had not been called into question earlier in the story, so the decree protecting the name of the Jewish God would seem to have been unnecessary. Two reasons for it can been recognized. It continues the emphasis on the power of the king. He had been thwarted for a moment, but quickly takes charge again by making this God the subject of one of his own severe orders. So the Jewish God has become "naturalized." Jewish readers would have taken the story more positively, for it says that pagan rulers may recognize and formally legalize their right to live as a people with distinct customs and beliefs. This did happen under the Persians and Ptolemies, and when he occupied Palestine in 199 BC, Antiochus III issued a decree confirming the right of the Jews to live according to their own laws (Josephus, *Antiquities of the Jews,* 12.3). Even though the pagan king is depicted in a more antagonistic way in this chapter than in the rest of chapters 1–6, the outlook as a whole corresponds to the other chapters in reflecting a time prior to the persecution under Antiochus IV Epiphanes.

Theological and Ethical Analysis

Both the literary and the exegetical analyses have noted the ways the story emphasizes Nebuchadnezzar's power. Shadrach, Meshach, and Abednego are true heroes, with their one speech the most important part of this chapter, but they are passive figures surrounded—at the beginning and the end—by authoritative decrees and threats of violence. The chapter thus reflects the painful reality minority groups must cope with. Put bluntly, they cannot do much. In the background are, we have been reminded, the high offices held by the three Jews, but we are not even offered a hint of what their accomplishments might be. This, unlike the court wise man stories that emphasize the success of the minority figure, is a different kind of tale. It speaks of life under claims to absolute power, and as such it is far from a "Sunday school story." Nebuchadnezzar's effort to punish the Jews is thwarted indeed, and that is important. But he does not suffer for his idolatry or cruelty. The theme of judgment is not present here, but will appear in chapters 4 and 5. He is as powerful at the end as at the beginning, but Jews are free to be Jews, and that is the modest (?) hope with which the chapter concludes.

In the story there is much that cannot be called realistic, but at its heart is a very sober realism concerning the fortunes of a minority people. If all goes well, they will live their own lives without much interference, but the major decisions that affect their lives are being made by someone else. At the end of this story, Shadrach, Meshach, and Abednego have been promoted, but the golden image is still there and Nebuchadnezzar is still in charge, so very little has changed concerning the conditions under which they have to live. Who knows when the next crisis will come?

This reemphasizes the point that the most important part of the story is not the happy ending but the center, that bold affirmation: "But if not, be it known to you, O king, that we will not serve your gods and we will not worship the golden statue that you have set up" (v. 18). The true heroism of the three is revealed in their discovery that it makes no difference to them whether they die or not, if their deaths are brought about because of their faithfulness to the God they serve. Earlier it was said that they did the right thing simply because it was right, but that is a bit too abstract. The personal element is essential: they refused to recognize any power greater than God, because he was their God.

"Does Job fear God for nothing?" the accuser asked God (Job 1:9). Job had been well rewarded for his righteousness, and the accuser implies there is no other reason for a person to be righteous. His question hangs over the rest of that book, and is partly answered by Job's insistence on maintaining his integrity (*tummâ*, 2:3, 9; 27:5); but it remains as a question that readers must answer for themselves. The Bible, New Testament included, speaks often of God's rewards for those who obey him, but even Proverbs, with its customary optimism, recognized that material rewards are not the highest aim in life: "Better the poor walking in integrity than one perverse of speech who is a fool" (Prov 19:1). The importance of the right motive for one's behavior appears in perhaps its most striking way in Dan 3:17-18, and it became an important part of Jewish teaching. Antigonus of Soko (early second century BC, near the time the book of Daniel was completed) is quoted as saying, "Be not like slaves that minister to the master for the sake of receiving a bounty, but be like slaves that minister to the master not for the sake of receiving a bounty; and let the fear of Heaven be upon you" (*Pirke Aboth* 1.3). The true motive for the keeping of the Law ought to be the love of God: "Let all thy deeds be done for the sake of Heaven" (*Pirke Aboth* 2.12).

At about the time the book of Daniel was completed, a form of reward not contemplated by the Old Testament authors appeared (as in 2 Macc 7 and Wis 3:1-9), namely the resurrection of the dead to eternal life. It is affirmed briefly in Dan 12:2, but plays no role in reassuring Shadrach, Meshach, and Abednego, or Daniel in chapter 6, as they face death. These stories thus confront the reader in the most forceful way with the question, "Do you *need* to be rewarded for doing what is right?"

George Adam Smith wrote of the Atheism of Force and the Atheism of Fear in his commentary on Isaiah (Smith 1928, 1: 171-82). Dan 3 can be read as a good example of the points Smith made, for Nebuchadnezzar's rhetorical question "Who is the god that will deliver you out of my hands?" represents the Atheism of Force. Once one possesses enough material power, the temptation is very strong to believe one no longer needs to be *responsible* to anyone else. There is an abundance of examples of that in world history, and not only in the absolute monarchies and dictatorships. On the other hand, the wielding of apparently absolute power may persuade those against whom it is wielded that it really is absolute, and that they have no resource to withstand it—the Atheism of Fear. Stories such as Dan 3 have insisted there is such a resource (in this case without explaining it), and that surely accounts for the popularity of the book among communities of the oppressed throughout the centuries. They have known there is not always a happy ending (as already the second-century Jews who made this a part of Holy Scripture knew), but the book of Daniel has served its subversive purpose of insisting that the Atheism of Force is a fraud.

DANIEL 4

The king's power, which was emphasized so strongly in chapter 3, is not rejected in this chapter, but its source is clarified. By means of a severe lesson, Nebuchadnezzar learns that he rules only by permission of the Most High God.

Literary Analysis

The structure of this chapter is more complex than that of the other stories, since it uses the "epistle" or public proclamation as a framework for another court wise man story. The verse numbering of English versions will be used here, since they make a proper division between chapters 3 and 4. When the Vulgate was divided into chapters and verses in the Middle Ages, Nebuchadnezzar's proclamation (4:1-3, English) was made the conclusion of chapter 3, and printed editions of the Masoretic Text follow that division to this day. However, there is general agreement that the story begins with the proclamation, as the English versions indicate.

Commentators have often been puzzled as to why Daniel is called in last (v. 8a) rather than being consulted first, since his superior wisdom is already known to Nebuchadnezzar (vv. 8b-9). This can be easily explained if we accept the pattern of the court wise man story as the form deliberately chosen by the author for the central structure of his narrative. Most of the pattern is here: the king is central, he faces a serious dilemma, his counselors are unsuccessful, then the true wise man appears. Daniel is not really an outsider this time, but the familiar pattern requires him to appear after the others have failed. Missing is the usual conclusion, his reward, but this is explained by the fact that the answer to the usual question, "Who is wisest?" is taken for granted, and the story is being used for another purpose, namely the fulfillment of Daniel's interpretation by the humiliation of Nebuchadnezzar.

Various explanations have been offered for the change from first person to third person at verse 19, then back to first person at verse 34. Since the court wise man story was always told in the third person, that would have been the natural way to relate the main part of the chapter, even though its structure has been elaborated by the introduction of a royal proclamation, which must be in the first person. One might guess that redactorial work took an original story in the third person and added the first-person framework without making many changes in the original, but that sort of reconstruction is speculative.

As in chapter 2, the king's dilemma results from a portentous dream, so the procedures of dream interpretation appear once again. The new element in this story is the account of how the dream was fulfilled, and that changes significantly the intent of the court wise man story. The climax now does not focus on the wise man, but on the king, whose change as a result of the dream and its fulfillment is the point of the narrative.

Nebuchadnezzar indulges in poetry as he praises the Most High God in verses 3, 34-35, and 37, and his description of the cosmic tree and its fate in verses 10-12 and 14-17 also takes poetic form, so there is considerable stylistic variety in this chapter as compared with the others. Repetition is evident, but used in a way different from chapter 3. Instead of lists, Nebuchadnezzar's description of the tree is repeated with some variation by Daniel, even though it is not necessary, since the details are not explained. "It is you, O king!" (v. 22) is the extent of the interpretation. The dehumanization of Nebuchadnezzar is repeated twice more, in verses 31 and 33, but this is necessary, since the story leads up to the fulfillment of the dream as its climax.

The dream of a great tree that reached to the heavens, providing shelter and food for all living beings, is based on the myth of the cosmic tree, one of the most common of all religious symbols (Eliade 1958, 265-330; James 1966). It is a way of imagining the entire cosmos, connecting heaven and the netherworld by its upper branches and its roots, while the shade of its branches is depicted as the place of habitation for all creatures. The world tree was described at length in Norse mythology (Turville-Petre 1964, 244-46, 279), but the presence of many of the same ideas in the Middle East is indicated in brief references in many texts as well as in iconography (Danthine 1937; Perrot 1937). For example, some Akkadian incantations associate various species of trees with the great cosmic tree:

> Incantation: Juniper, growing from the sprout!
> Young Juniper, growing from the sprout!
> juniper whose boughs (and) intertwining branches are precious,
> great pillar of heaven, great foundation of earth,
> resplendent doorpost of Enlil, strong lock of the temple of Enlil.
> (Reiner 1958, 46)

Some "naturalistic" scenes in Assyrian art may almost be taken as illustrations of the myth, since they depict a tree with gazelles under it and birds above (Parrot 1961, 146; Perrot 1937, plate 11, figure 52).

A rather full description of the world tree appears in Ezek 31, where it is put to a new use by the prophet (Gowan 1975, 93-116). The tree, which represents stability and security, as one would like the world to be, is identified with the king of Egypt: "Whom are you like in your greatness? . . . Which among the trees of Eden was like you in glory and in greatness?" (31:2, 18). Ezekiel seems to acknowledge the real power and wealth of the pharaoh, but then he has the cosmic tree cut down, something that has no parallel in Near Eastern mythology. Since the tree represents the king, he even has it descend into Sheol, a strange thing to say of a tree, but he is willing to use the imagery very freely, as is also done in Daniel 4.

Numerous partial parallels to the dream in Dan 4 have been cited, many of them rather remote, but the relationship between this chapter and Ezek 31 is so close that it seems evident that the author of Daniel knew Ezekiel's use of the mythological theme, and used it again in a similar way, with direct echoes of some of the language. In each case the symbol of the tree is a positive indication of the king's greatness (Dan 4:22), and in each case the original meaning of the myth has been broken, when the great tree is cut down.

There is general agreement that this chapter is related in some way to traditions about king Nabonidus, the last king of the Neo-Babylonian empire. A fragmentary text found in Cave 4 at Qumran (4QPrNab) has even led to the claim that it contains the "original" form of the story recorded in Dan 4. What remains of the text introduces it as a prayer said by Nabonidus when he was afflicted with boils in Teiman (the oasis in northern Arabia where he spent ten years at the end of his reign). According to the text, he suffered for seven years then was pardoned. A Jewish diviner was somehow involved (Jongeling, Labuschagne, and van der Woude 1976, 121-31). There are three or four parallels: a Babylonian king is afflicted for seven years and is involved with a Jew identified by a word (*gzr*, "diviner") that also appears in Dan 4:7. The differences are significant: although the name of a lesser-known king might well have been replaced by the famous Nebuchadnezzar, the affliction is different, and there is no evidence of a dream interpreted by the Jew, or of the theme of the cosmic tree. Knowing that Nabonidus had a bad reputation and was accused of strange behavior ("Verse Account of Nabonidus," Pritchard 1955, 312-15), it is reasonable to think that both texts may have originated in some of the negative traditions about him, but they are different enough that caution suggests no direct relationship should be affirmed.

Exegetical Analysis

The Royal Proclamation (4:1-3)

The form of these three verses of the story follows the usual pattern of letters in the ancient Near East, beginning with the name of the sender and the addressee(s), followed by a greeting (note the letters in Ezra 4:11; 7:12). This is not a private letter, but a public pronouncement of a type that is familiar, especially from Assyrian inscriptions. The usual contents boast of the king's accomplishments, but give the gods credit for the power he possesses; so verse 2 fits the pattern, except that divine names are missing (cf. the inscriptions of Esarhaddon and Xerxes in Pritchard 1955, 289, 316). The bit of poetry in verse 3 introduces the new theme to come, however, which differs from chapter 3, where Nebuchadnezzar's power was emphasized. The emphasis in this chapter will be the power of the Most High.

The Ominous Dream (4:4-18)

An expanded form of the court wise man story, very similar to the one in chapter 2 except for the demand that the sages reveal the dream on threat of death, appears in verses 4-27. Only Daniel's reward is missing, and that is because of the new elements that follow. The disturbing effects of this dream are emphasized by Nebuchadnezzar's reminder that he had been at ease and prospering. As in chapter 2 a list of the various specialists in dream interpretation is provided (v. 4), but their failure is passed over quickly. Daniel must appear after they have been unsuccessful, for that is the way these stories are told; but he is clearly well known to Nebuchadnezzar, from the way he is described in verse 8 and addressed in verse 9.

Now the king relates his dream of the cosmic tree in words strongly reminiscent of Ezek 31. The first new element is the appearance of a "watcher" *(ʿîr)*, a holy one who comes down from heaven to call for the felling of the great tree (v. 13). This is the only place in the Masoretic Text where this word is used of heavenly beings, but it became widely used in the Jewish literature of the hellenistic and Roman periods. In another work produced near the time of Daniel, *1 Enoch* 1–36, the term is often used of fallen angels, but it also introduces the names of the seven archangels as the "holy angels who watch" (*1 Enoch* 20:1). The texts do not explain what they are to "watch," unless it be over human affairs, as the *satan* was to do in Job 1–2 (for a full discussion, see Collins 1993, 224-25).

In Ezek 31 God announces through the prophet the thorough destruction of the great tree and makes it explicit that this is judgment for overweening pride. The Hebrew words for height are also used to denote pride (cf. "haughty" in English), so the great height of the tree made it a good symbol for the pharaoh's pride, which Ezekiel condemned. Words of judgment do not appear at this point in Dan 4, however, and the tone of the whole chapter is milder than that of Ezek 31. In both chapters a shocking use is made of the cosmic tree, for it is no longer a place of shelter for living beings. In Daniel, however, it does not die, for the destruction is to have a corrective effect, and so we are told that the stump and roots are left with a band of iron and bronze (v. 15).

The band around the stump is not explained. It has been suggested that it really refers to the binding of the king in his madness, but that is unlikely, since nothing is said of binding him in the fulfillment, when he roams the fields with the animals (vv. 23, 32-33). The many depictions of sacred trees in Assyrian art are highly schematic, so it is hard to tell how they were decorated, but the excavation of the Shamash temple at Khorsabad found a tree trunk with two skillfully embossed bronze bands around it (Loud 1936, 104). This verse may thus be a passing reference to such sacred trees.

Without warning, in verses 15*b*-16, the tree has become a man, and its felling represents the change from humanity to sharing the lot of animals. This is in keeping with the theme of reversal of fortune that is typical of the *"hybris*-texts" in the Old Testament. The king of Babylon who thought he could ascend above the stars of God in Isa 14:4-21 is brought down to the netherworld, awesome power turned to utter helplessness. The king of Tyre, called "full of wisdom and perfect in beauty," comes to such a dreadful end that the peoples are appalled at him (Ezek 28:11-19). And the Egyptian king, once glorified as the cosmic tree itself, will lie down in Sheol with the uncircumcised and those slain by the sword (Ezek 31). Note that each of these texts is more extreme than Dan 4. Nebuchadnezzar is changed from a man to an animal, but only for "seven times" (probably years, since "time" is used that way in 7:25), but the fate of these other kings is death (see the theological analysis). The reason given for Nebuchadnezzar's chastisement does not refer to any of his sins, remarkably enough, but emphasizes the primary theme of the chapter (already alluded to in v. 3): "The Most High is sovereign over the kingdom of mortals" (v. 17). It is the theme developed at length by Second Isaiah in exile: "Never mind the displays of earthly power around you. There is a God greater than all this, and a Nebuchadnezzar or a Cyrus rules only at his sufferance. Try to believe it if you can."

Interpretation (4:19-27)

Daniel's distress when he hears the dream has been variously understood. Some see him as worrying about his own fate when he must give the king bad news, but that does not fit his character as he appears in the other stories. Elsewhere he is depicted as a loyal servant of the kings for whom he works, and this is probably the reason for his gracious words here. Oppenheim points out that it was customary for the interpreter to wish something favorable for the dreamer (Oppenheim 1956, 205; see Gen 41:16). Jewish exegetes in the past were quite disturbed by "may the dream be for those who hate you" (v. 19), saying Daniel seems to be turning the dream against his own people, and they sought another way to read it.

The meaning of the dream was clear without much interpretation, so Daniel essentially repeats it, with one necessary addition: "It is you, O king!" explaining that the world tree represents his greatness that reaches to heaven and to the ends of the earth

(v. 22). There is some evidence in ancient Near Eastern art and texts that kings may have been identified with a sacred tree of one kind or another, so the move made in Ezek 31 and Dan 4 may not have been surprising (see the references noted earlier). One text is worth citing here as a parallel to what Daniel says of Nebuchadnezzar. He described his empire as a great tree: "Under her everlasting shadow I gathered all men in peace. A reign of abundance, years of plenty I caused to be in my land" (Nebuchadnezzar's inscription at the Wady Brissa; Langdon 1905, 171).

Having repeated the dream, Daniel adds some advice, suggesting the chastisement might be averted (v. 27). Nebuchadnezzar's sins and iniquities are now mentioned for the first and only time in the chapter. Righteousness and mercy are called for, with an interesting choice of the verb, *prq*, literally "break off" (used only here in biblical Aramaic). It may have the sense of throwing off the burden or the bonds of sins. There has been extended discussion of the word "righteousness" in this context, since the word eventually came to mean almsgiving, and the verse was thought to indicate one could pay for one's sins by charity. The word never means almsgiving in the Old Testament, and that is not the meaning of the Aramaic sentence.

The Fulfillment (4:28-37)

Without explanation, there was a twelve-month interval between the dream and its fulfillment, and the occasion as described was a relatively mild boast on Nebuchadnezzar's part, concerning his prowess as the builder of Babylon. His actual building inscriptions are more extravagant:

> Nebuchadrezzar, king of BABYLON, whom MERODACH, the great Lord, for the weal of his city BABYLON did call, am I. ESAGILLA and EZIDA like the brilliance of the sun I made shine. The temples of the great gods like day I made bright. . . . Silver, gold, precious stones, everything that is prized, is magnificent; substance, wealth, the ornaments of majesty, I heaped up within it; strength, splendour, royal treasure, I hoarded within it." (Sayce 1890, 117, 119)

Daniel 4 does not depict Nebuchadnezzar in as pejorative a way as one might expect. But the boast is sufficient to bring the threatened chastisement upon him, and it all comes true as predicted.

Nebuchadnezzar's fate has been compared with the psychological condition called lycanthropy, in which people believe themselves to be animals and behave accordingly; but the author of Daniel was no student of abnormal psychology, and there is no evidence in the career of Nebuchadnezzar that he was actually disabled for any significant period of time. The meaning of the bizarre behavior attributed to him should thus be interpreted theologically rather than psychologically. The text wants to say that the result of seeking to become more than human is the loss of humanity—the reversal-of-fortune theme. "Man is neither angel nor beast, and the mischief is that he who would play the angel plays the beast" (Pascal 1950, 90-91).

Since the intention of the chastisement was to teach Nebuchadnezzar that "the Most High has sovereignty over the kingdom of mortals, and gives it to whom he will" (v. 25), the fulfillment of the dream includes his acceptance of that truth. Having regained his humanity, Nebuchadnezzar is allowed to speak in the first person once more (vv. 34-37). He acknowledges the sovereignty of the Most High in poetry (vv. 34-35) but, having been restored to the throne, claims that still more greatness was added to him (verse 36). The story thus has a very different end from the similar prophetic texts noted earlier. The legitimacy of pagan kingship is not denied, but is even affirmed to be the will of the Most High God, although completely subject to his will. Finally, Nebuchadnezzar praises God for his truth and justice (attributes the great kings always claimed for themselves), but the point the prophets had made about kingship does appear at the very end: "He is able to bring low those who walk in pride."

Theological and Ethical Analysis

Allusions to ancient Near Eastern myths appear occasionally in the Old Testament, but the most extensive use of mythological themes is restricted to passages dealing with foreign kings. In Isa 14:12-14 the prophet boldly takes up the story of the younger god who attempts to usurp the throne of the high god, and identifies the king of Babylon as such a god. His attempt to become "like the Most High" leads to a shameful death, however. In 28:12-19 Ezekiel identified the king of Tyre with the first man in the Garden of Eden, and we have already noted his identification of the pharaoh with the cosmic tree. In each of these texts the very impressive accomplishments of great kings are acknowledged by associating them with myths dealing with power, wealth, and wisdom. But the prophets recognized a danger that comes with the possession of almost absolute power (possible for kings then, and for dictators and the technological society today), namely the feeling that "almost" absolute power is not enough. It is tempting to refuse to accept any limits on one's power, and thus to feel responsible to no one. The prophets recognized that, and, without denying the accomplishments of the great nations, called that final claim a rebellion against God that would lead inevitably to death. The same theme appears in Ps 82:6-8:

> I say, "You are gods,
> children of the Most High, all of you;
> nevertheless, you shall die like mortals,
> and fall like any prince."
> Rise up, O God, judge the earth;
> for all the nations belong to you!

Bertrand Russell wrote: "Every man would like to be God, if it were possible; some few find it difficult to admit the impossibility" (Russell 1938, 11). His statement is more relevant to the state than it is to individuals, because of the immense power available to the governments of great nations. The prophets spoke of kings because in their day they were "the state"; but their mythologizing of the state's claims fits the modern nation as well as (or better than) it fit Egypt or Babylon (for a full study of the subject, see Gowan 1975).

These kings were religious men, of course, and certainly did not think of themselves as rebels against the gods. Indeed, they claimed that they ruled because the gods had chosen them, and their successes were evidence of the gods' blessings. To the prophets, they were simply mistaken in that, for they were responsible to the God of Israel, whether they knew it or not.

"Have you not heard
    that I determined it long ago?
I planned from days of old
    what now I bring to pass,
that you should make fortified cities
    crash into heaps of ruins."
(Isa 37:26; an oracle against Sennacherib; see also Isa 10:5-19)

I call you by your name,
    I surname you, though you do not know me.
I am the LORD, and there is no other;
    besides me there is no god.
I arm you, though you do not know me.
                     (Isa 45:4b-5; of Cyrus)

These are the audacious claims made for the God of the tiny nation of Judah, which had even ceased to exist by the time of Second Isaiah and Daniel. But chapter 4 takes up this theme from the prophets and tells a story that claims their predictions came to a kind of fulfillment in Nebuchadnezzar himself. There is a ferocity about the prophetic passages that is largely missing from this story, however. Nebuchadnezzar's sins are alluded to once but are not specified. Language concerning his greatness, also part of the prophetic texts, appears prominently (vv. 22, 30, 36). He suffers a degrading experience, but he does not die; indeed he becomes even greater after his restoration. This reflects an attitude toward foreign rule quite different from Second Isaiah's opinion of Babylon, as it appears in Isa 47.

Nebuchadnezzar is not "converted," however. He does not learn the name of Daniel's God, let alone any Israelite theology. Daniel does not teach him anything. Nebuchadnezzar has learned and now acknowledges with some enthusiasm that the "Most High" whom he identifies with Daniel's God (but all religions have a most high god) is more powerful than he and is actually the source of his power.

The story thus contains the rather modest hopes of a group of monotheists whose daily lives seem to be completely under the control of the government of a great empire. Life is not unbearable for them—again we think of the Persian and Ptolemaic periods. The desire to be freed from oppressive rule does not appear, as it does in chapters 7–12. But the obvious dominance of the pagan government continues to raise the question that had bothered the prophets long ago: Who is really in charge here? Could it possibly be Yahweh, the God of a defeated people? This story, in which that God, whose name Nebuchadnezzar does not even know, interferes with his very mind, was intended to reassure the Jewish minority, wherever they lived, that Yahweh is sovereign, after all. As far as we know, there was never any such hiatus in Nebuchadnezzar's reign, but the story is realistic to this extent: Nebuchadnezzar does not become a true Yahwist. To do that would create a situation in the narrative which did not correspond to life as the readers knew it. Their story involved continuing to live under a pagan king, as Daniel does, but they needed to know there is another king.

Perhaps the real Nebuchadnezzar was not convinced the Jewish God was lord of all. What does that say about the truth of the story? History does provide some confirmation of what it wants to say. Babylon the great lies in ruins, great empires rise and fall, Napoleon and Hitler are just bad memories, but the people of that Jewish God live on.

DANIEL 5

Nebuchadnezzar is gone and now Belshazzar is king in this story concerning the end of the Neo-Babylonian empire. The story is told with no reference to armies, but only as the account of the death of a king, and his replacement. This chapter introduces two of the major historical problems of the book of Daniel, since what is said of Belshazzar does not correspond with Babylonian and Persian records, and there is no place in those records for a Darius the Mede.

Literary Analysis

This court wise man story is less complex than the stories in chapters 2 and 4. After an introduction briefly describing Belshazzar's feast, during which the vessels from the Jerusalem temple were used in connection with adoration of idols, the dilemma appears immediately, in the form of mysterious writing on the wall rather than as a dream. The distress the writing causes is emphasized more than usual, then the unsuccessful counselors appear. The development of the plot is then delayed considerably by speeches of the queen and the king which serve eventually to introduce the true wise man (vv. 10-16). Daniel delays the story even more with an accusatory speech, the most important new element in the chapter (vv. 17-23), then the conclusion is stated very concisely with the interpretation, the reward, and the fulfillment. Whereas the fulfillment in chapter 4 occupied ten verses, in this chapter it is one short and dramatic sentence.

The basic plot has been expanded mostly by speeches. Chapter 4 introduced an element from the prophetic books—the theme of overweening pride of great kings, expressed by the use of the myth of the cosmic tree. Here Daniel's speech is more like the words of the prophets than anything else in the book. The book itself does not identify Daniel as a prophet, and he does not use the familiar forms "Thus says the Lord" and "oracle of the Lord," but the recollection of past history (vv. 18-21), the citation of present sins (vv. 22-23), and the announcement of judgment (vv. 24-28) is a pattern reminiscent of the prophetic books.

Belshazzar should be the center of the story, but, as depicted, he has little personality. We are not told why he called for and used the sacred vessels, and realistic reaction to Daniel's message is not attributed to him. His only human trait appears in the detailed and repeated description of the symptoms of his panic at seeing the words on the wall (vv. 6, 9, and 10). That is appropriate, for, more than any of the characters, it is the mysterious writing that dominates the story.

Exegetical Analysis

Introduction: The Banquet (5:1-4)

The story begins abruptly without any indication as to how Belshazzar became king or whether there was any special occasion for the banquet. Speculation has made it his coronation feast, or a feast associated with the Babylonian New Year observance, or a last fling before the city fell to the enemy; but nothing like this is of interest to the storyteller. He moves immediately to what concerns him, the use of sacred vessels from the Jerusalem temple for drinking wine at a pagan feast in association with praise for the Babylonian idols. Belshazzar's motive for using the vessels has been supplied by interpreters, but here again the narrator is silent. All that matters to the story is what Belshazzar did, not why (note vv. 22-23). The vessels were all that remained of worship in the Temple, so their expropriation by Nebuchadnezzar (2 Kgs 25:14-15) and their return by the order of Cyrus (Ezra 1:7-11) were important events. Recall that the reference to the vessels in Dan 1:2 serves as an introduction to this chapter. This concern for the Temple makes the outlook of chapter 5 a bit different from the other stories, since they focus entirely on life in exile, without reference to the promised land or Jerusalem. Here the crime of Belshazzar that will lead immediately to his death is disrespect for cult objects, which for the exiles is all that remains of the Temple.

Two apparent historical errors have already appeared: Belshazzar is called king, and Nebuchadnezzar is called his father. The latter is certainly not true. Belshazzar was the son of Nabonidus, who usurped the throne in 556, so Belshazzar was not even related to Nebuchadnezzar. And he had not succeeded Nabonidus as king. During the king's ten-year sojourn in Teima (alluded to in the commentary on chap. 4), Belshazzar did serve as regent in Babylon, but the contemporary texts always refer to him as "son of the king," not "king." The date formulas use Nabonidus's name, and the New Year festival in which the king had to play a central role did not take place, since Nabonidus was not present (Pritchard 1955, 306, 313-16). The proposal that Belshazzar's mother *might* have been Nebuchadnezzar's daughter has no evidence to support it. The story evidently was formulated at a time when it could be assumed Belshazzar was king, since it was remembered he was managing affairs in Babylon shortly before it passed into the hands of the Persians, and when the transfer of rule from Nebuchadnezzar's family to Nabonidus had been forgotten.

The Writing on the Wall (5:5-9)

Having introduced the king as the central character, the narrative moves to the next two elements of the typical wisdom story: an omen that upsets Belshazzar, and the inability of his wise men to interpret it. The effect it had on him is more extreme than the effect of the dreams on Nebuchadnezzar, as well it might be—not only to see letters appear on the wall but also to see them being written by a disembodied hand! His tremors are followed by a loud cry to summon the usual diviners, and he offers them a fabulous reward, so his dignity, if any at that point in a drinking bout, has been seriously disrupted. The counselors fail, as we knew they would, and we are told again of his terror (v. 9). The challenge the diviners faced was twofold, and that seems important for understanding Daniel's accomplishment. It was to "read this writing and tell me its interpretation" (v. 7). This has fired the imagination of scholars, leading to a range of theories to explain why they could not read the writing. A Jewish tradition assumed the writing was in the Aramaic alphabet but written vertically rather than horizontally, so that it looked like gibberish (reproduced in Rembrandt's painting of the scene). More recently, the idea that some form of cuneiform appeared on the wall has been proposed, but the Chaldeans would have been able to read that. Usually the simplest answer is the best, and a simple answer will be offered here. The author was thinking of three or four words (see v. 25) written in the Aramaic alphabet, since that is what he was using, and of course without vowel points, since there were no such things in those days. The words did not obviously make a sentence, which would provide the clues as to what vowels to supply; so the "reading" meant knowing how to pronounce the words, thus what their grammatical forms were. Since this was obviously a supernatural message, it would be assumed that a second step would then be necessary—the interpretation of what was expected to be a hidden meaning in those words. The Chaldeans acknowledge failure at both tasks.

The Queen Intervenes and Daniel Is Introduced (5:10-16)

The development of the plot is delayed now, telling readers what they already know about Daniel—twice (vv. 11-12 and

13-14). All interpreters agree that the queen who now appears must be the queen mother rather than Belshazzar's wife, since she seems to have a longer memory than he does. She follows court protocol, addressing him "O king, live forever!" but takes it upon herself to advise him in a way that seems more likely to come from his mother than his wife. The prestige of the queen mother in oriental courts is well documented (see 1 Kgs 1:15-21; 24:12; Ezek 19).

Belshazzar seems not to know that his own father (according to the story) had appointed Daniel to be chief of the magicians, enchanters, Chaldeans, and diviners (Dan 2:48). Is Daniel supposedly no longer serving in that capacity? We are not told, but the queen mother extols his qualities, piling up wisdom vocabulary: "enlightenment, understanding, and wisdom" (v. 11) and "knowledge, and understanding to interpret dreams, explain riddles, and solve problems" (v. 12). She advises Belshazzar to call Daniel and he does so. Her intervention makes it possible for the story to run as it should, with Daniel playing the role of outsider again in spite of the position he held under Nebuchadnezzar.

When the king sees Daniel, he seems to know something about him, since he identifies him as one of the exiles from Judah— unless we are to assume he just learned this from his mother, and the author omitted it from her speech. He repeats Daniel's special qualifications and offers him the same magnificent reward, if he can read and interpret the writing on the wall.

Daniel's Oration (5:17-23)

The movement of the plot is delayed again. Daniel delivers a speech reminiscent of the oracles of the prophets, although nowhere in the book is he identified as a prophet, and he does not use typical formulas such as "Thus says the Lord." Unlike the queen, Daniel ignores proper etiquette and bluntly refuses to show any interest in rewards (v. 17).

His speech has two parts, three when the interpretation of the omen is included. First he recounts Nebuchadnezzar's experience of being degraded to the state of an animal (see chap. 4; the most extensive connection made between any two chapters in the book), which taught him that "the Most High has sovereignty over the kingdom of mortals" (vv. 18-21). Then he points out that Belshazzar has learned nothing, that his use of the Temple vessels meant exalting himself against the Lord of heaven. The most explicit anti-idolatry words of the book appear in verse 23, "which do not see or hear or know." But Belshazzar has honored those gods of silver, gold, bronze, iron, wood, and stone rather than the God who gives him his very breath.

The Interpretation and Its Fulfillment (5:24-31)

Daniel's speech follows the pattern of the familiar "reason-announcement oracle" of the prophetic books (e.g., Isa 37:29; Ezek 29:9b-12; Amos 5:11). The "reason" portion, his accusation (vv. 17-23) is now followed by an announcement of impending judgment, in the form of an interpretation of the mysterious words. He reads them then derives a message from each of them.

The text is puzzling, since the explanation in verse 26 makes no reference to *měnēʾ* being repeated in verse 25, and the form of the final word is different in verses 25 and 28. The versions support reading *měnēʾ*, *těqēl*, and *pěrēs* in verse 25, to correspond with verses 26-28, and most commentators agree. The repetition of *měnēʾ* could be accounted for as a result of dittography, but a basic principle of text criticism counsels preference for the more difficult reading, which is the Masoretic Text. It may be that very early translators "corrected" verse 25 to make it agree with verses 26-28, as modern scholars do. It would not be necessary for Daniel's interpretation to agree with the exact form of the words on the wall, given the way Middle Eastern authors dealt with this kind of thing. Commentators now regularly note that the Habakkuk Commentary found at Qumran quotes the biblical text one way in 12:1, then comments on a slightly different form of it in 12:6. In Gen 22:14, Abraham names the mountain Yahweh-Yireh, using the active form of the verb, but the author explains the name as if the passive had been used. The author of Gen 18:9-15 surely intends us to think of Isaac's name, "he laughs," when he, without worrying about the difference in gender, tells us that Sarah laughed. Ahiqar is given riddles to solve by the king of

Egypt, and his feats would not impress any of us, but they have some relationship to the problem set and are clever, which is the most important matter (Charles 1913, 2:764-65). The evidence indicates that exact correspondence was of no interest to the authors of any of these stories.

Almost every commentator insists that these words originally must have meant something different from what Daniel said they did. The favorite theory is that they were pronounced as the names of weights, that is, mina, shekel, and half (mina or shekel?), then various interpretations of the weights are offered as value judgments with reference to one king or another. Another approach adds different vowels to the consonants so as to make a sentence of them. One can almost see the commentators in a semicircle, looking over the shoulders of the Chaldeans, and puzzling over those cryptic words as if Daniel had never showed up—but with more confidence than the Chaldeans that they had really deciphered the message. The motive for their efforts is stated in Hartman and Di Lella: "It would be strange, however, if the three words had no meaning in themselves, other than the puns that Daniel sees in them" (Hartman and Di Lella 1978, 189; later acknowledging the speculative nature of all the efforts, p. 190). Long ago, Montgomery quoted C. C. Torrey with approval, but few have taken these scholars seriously. Torrey wrote: "The man who wrote this tale *must* be supposed to have known what the solution was. It is quite necessary that Belshazzar and his magicians should have been mystified by the inscription; but it certainly requires desperate courage to reject the interpretation given us by the author of the story, and defend another in total conflict with it" (Torrey 1909, 277; partly quoted in Montgomery 1927, 262). Taking Torrey's advice, let us assume that the author knew what he was writing, and that since he wrote in Aramaic he was thinking of three or four clusters of consonants in the Aramaic script. They were certainly unpointed in the early manuscripts, so the reader, like the Chaldeans, would not have known what to make of them until Daniel explained them. Torrey imagines how such a reader would have tried various possibilities (Torrey 1909, 280). Eventually, a tradition developed as to how they should be pronounced so that the Daniel scroll could be read aloud. (Almost all reading, even for private purposes, was done aloud in antiquity.) The tradition is early, since the ancient versions all support the pointing of the Masoretic Text, which makes nouns of the words. Daniel, according to that tradition, first reads them as nouns then uses them as verbs, which has troubled scholars but would not have been seen as a problem in antiquity.

The straightforward reading of the text thus finds a group of ambiguous consonants on the wall, and the point of the mysterious writing is that the words, even when pronounced by Daniel, still mean nothing until he gives them meaning. He pronounces them as nouns (Montgomery 1927, 262), then makes a verbal sentence of them.

NUMBER *(mĕnē˒)*: God has numbered the days of your kingdom and brought it to an end (v. 26).
WEIGHT *(tĕqēl)*: You have been weighed on the scales and found wanting (v. 27).
DIVISION *(pĕrēs)*: Your kingdom is divided and given to the Medes and Persians (v. 28).

This unconditional announcement of judgment receives a strange response from Belshazzar. His terror ought to have been redoubled, but now nothing is said of any emotion. The story continues as court wise man stories are supposed to do, with the rewarding of Daniel. Then comes an abrupt ending, the fulfillment of the omen that very night.

Here are more historical problems: Belshazzar's father, Nabonidus, returned from Teima to Babylon in 543 and resumed his full duties as king (Beaulieu 1995, 976). Belshazzar disappeared from administrative texts at that point, so it is clear he was not even serving as *de facto* king in 539 when the Persians occupied Babylon. "That very night" (v. 30) is vague, of course, and may refer to a tradition that Belshazzar was murdered at some time of which we have no record. What is clear from the contemporary records is that when Babylon fell, Nabonidus was king, the city was occupied without a fight, Nabonidus was arrested (to be released later), and "the kingdom" came under the suzerainty of Cyrus the Persian, not Darius the Mede (for more on the problem of Darius, see the commentary on chap. 6).

Theological and Ethical Analysis

The point of the court wise man story appears again, and it is familiar to those who have read chapters 1, 2, and 4. The one true God is the only source of true wisdom, and he graciously makes that available to those who are faithful to him. Daniel claimed it and the king acknowledged it in chapter 2, the narrator states it in chapter 1, it appears briefly from the mouth of the king in chapter 4, and here both queen and king acknowledge it. The wisdom plot is used in this chapter as the framework for another point, which is introduced by Belshazzar's treatment of the holy vessels, spelled out in Daniel's speech and confirmed at the story's end. This is a story of divine judgment of a pagan king for failure to honor the one true God, leading to the death penalty.

The crime is not one we would have expected, given the setting, with Jews in exile, and a reminder that Nebuchadnezzar had sacked the Temple. The Neo-Babylonian empire is about to be turned over to Darius the Mede, but not for reasons cited in the prophetic words against Babylon (Isa 13–14; 47; Jer 50–51); namely, violence against the nations and overweening pride. The crime here is a cultic one, disrespectful treatment of sacred objects—associated, it is true, with idolatry. There are four specifications in Daniel's indictment (vv. 22-23): Belshazzar had exalted himself against the Lord of heaven; he and his company had drunk wine from the vessels of the Temple; he praised the gods of silver, and so forth; and he did not honor the God who gave him his very breath. For a Jew these would certainly have been most serious offenses, but what could be expected of a pagan? Daniel has an answer for that: Belshazzar should have learned from Nebuchadnezzar's experience (v. 22). But why would Daniel ignore the ways Jews had suffered under the Babylonians and focus instead on a ritual matter? It may be that at the heart of the story is the knowledge, among Babylonian Jews, of some scandalous treatment of those sacred objects; otherwise why would not the destruction of the Temple or continuance in exile have been more likely accusations? The very fact that the Temple vessels were still in captivity would have been a sensitive matter to Babylonian Jews, and some such occurrence might account for the appearance of this story, which follows the pattern of others in the Old Testament that speak of the immediate disastrous results of improper contact with holiness.

Uzzah put out his hands to steady the ark of the covenant when he thought it was in danger of falling, and he fell dead (2 Sam 6: 6-9). His motives were apparently innocent, but here holiness is depicted as dangerously powerful. Nadab and Abihu made an incense offering in a way that God had not commanded, and were struck down for violating the rules of holiness (Lev 10:1-3). King Uzziah also insisted on his independence in making an offering, and instantly became a leper (2 Chron 26:16-21). Somewhat later than Daniel, 2 Macc 3:4-40 recorded the efforts of Heliodorus to confiscate funds from the Jerusalem temple and the fact that he was saved from death only through the intercession of the high priest. Daniel 5 is the same type of story: almost instant death as a result of improper behavior with respect to the holy. As such, it seems far removed from the ethical issues raised by exile, issues that can easily be made meaningful to us. In one way it is an unusual theme for Dan 1–6, for only here and in 1:1-2 does Jerusalem play a role of any significance as Jews attempt to maintain their identity in exile. Noting this reminds us how different the stories in Daniel are from the prophetic books and the psalms, where Jerusalem plays a central role.

Daniel uses the cultic offense as a way of restating the main theme of the whole book, which remains of lasting importance. Jews living under governments capable of the lavish display of wealth with which this story began needed every possible assurance that the gods of those governments, whose temples were without doubt far more ornate than the one in Jerusalem, were not gods, after all. It could not have been easy to believe that Yahweh, their apparently defeated God, really was in charge. Ezekiel made the point in powerful prophetic language, Second Isaiah made it in impressive poetry, Daniel makes it with winsome stories. Daniel 5 is dramatic, with the handwriting on the wall, but it could have ended more dramatically, for with the end of Neo-Babylonian rule the point could have been emphasized—the gods of Nebuchadnezzar and Belshazzar could not save them. The author of the story very likely knew that the worship of the same gods was reestablished by Cyrus, however (Pritchard 1955, 316), and the Jews for whom he wrote continued to live under pagan kings; so the change, although significant, was not quite the evidence of the sovereignty of Yahweh that would have been hoped for. Those who read these books and believed the words, however, found that the words helped to keep faith alive. Something like that must happen for all who believe God really is active in human history. The evidence for it is not as clear-cut as we would wish, and there is a lot of evidence against it. The writers of Scripture believed they could see a hand at work in the midst of and behind the terrors of human affairs (and once, spelling it out on a wall), a hand guiding history not toward chaos but toward blessing. They may have been wrong—we cannot prove it—but belief in their testimony has sustained many for a long time.

DANIEL 6

A new king was introduced in Dan 5:31 (Masoretic Text, 6:1), and he remains one of the mysteries of the book. He is said to have received the kingdom after Belshazzar's death, and with no further explanation he appears as the central character in the next story, to be succeeded, according to 6:28, by Cyrus the Persian. He is identified further in 9:1 as "son of Ahasuerus, by birth a Mede, who became king over the realm of the Chaldeans." Unfortunately, in the contemporary records there is no evidence for the existence of such a person, and no room in the chronology for him between Belshazzar (or Nabonidus) and Cyrus.

Eventually there would be three kings named Darius, but they were Persians, not Medes, and Darius I (522–486) ruled after Cyrus and Cambyses. Cyrus the Persian became ruler of the Neo-Babylonian empire in 539, the year Babylon was occupied. Since there was a short interval between the occupation of the city by the

Persian army and Cyrus's arrival, a search has been made for someone who might have governed during that period and who might have been called Darius the Mede. The general, Gubaru (Greek: Gobryas), was a favorite candidate, but it is probable that he died shortly after the occupation, and it is known that Cambyses governed Babylon for his father, Cyrus. What would appear to be the last possible way to defend the historicity of this Darius the Mede is the claim that in 6:28, "the reign of Darius and the reign of Cyrus the Persian" really means "Darius, that is, Cyrus," and that the same king had not only two names but also two ethnic designations (Wiseman 1965, 9-16; defended by Shea 1991, 235-57). Cyrus's father was Cambyses I, a Persian (not Ahasuerus, as in 9:1), and although his mother, Mandane, was a Mede, it seems doubtful he would have been identified as "by birth a Mede." There is no explanation of why Cyrus might also have been known as Darius—and known by that name only to the author of Daniel.

Darius I had to occupy Babylon (in 520) after a period of unrest and was known for his administrative ability. It was he who organized the empire into satrapies (6:1), and he was remembered for his favorable treatment of the Jews (Ezra 4:24; 6; Haggai). He thus fits the picture of the king in Dan 6, but he was not a Mede and ruled well after Cyrus. If he was the original subject of the story, it must have taken its present form late enough that the chronology had been forgotten. The Prophets had said that the Medes would take Babylon (Isa 13:17; 21:1-10; Jer 51:11), and the familiar pattern of empires which located the Medes between Babylon (or Assyria) and Persia (see Dan 2:30) seems to have led the author of Daniel to identify his kings in the same sequence: Nebuchadnezzar and Belshazzar (Babylonian), Darius (Medes), and Cyrus (Persian).

Literary Analysis

This is a good example of the "legend of the faithful one in jeopardy." It is very similar to chapter 3, and has several parallels with chapter 1. As in chapter 3, danger arises because of a report to the king based on the Jews' insistence on practicing their religion. Their refusal to compromise results in a punishment that should have led to certain death, but they are saved by a miracle. The king then acknowledges the superiority of their God. The stories differ in several details. It is more obvious in chapter 6 that Daniel is the object of a conspiracy because of professional rivalry. The religious issue his opponents choose to focus on is not distinctively Jewish, as in chapter 3, for people of every religion pray. The king acts as Daniel's champion rather than as his accuser; thus there is no place in the story for a testimony comparable to that of Shadrach, Meshach, and Abednego (3:16-18). The most significant parallel between chapters 1 and 6 is the fact that only in these two chapters is the practice of a religious custom the focus of attention: diet in chapter 1, and prayer in chapter 6.

Two key words should be noted, since they point to the tension that runs through the story. The root $b^c h$ occurs five times as a verb (vv. 5, 8, 12-14) and twice as a noun (vv. 8, 14). It means "seek, request, pray," and as a noun "petition, prayer." The strange, broad interdict, "whoever petitions anyone for thirty days," thus traps Daniel because of his known practice of daily prayer. The Persian word $d\bar{a}t$ (order, law) occurs in verses 5, 8, 12, and 16, and identifies the issue that separates Daniel from his accusers. "We shall not find any ground for complaint against this Daniel unless we find it in connection with the law of his God" (v. 5). They do not select a practice of his that is unique to Judaism, so the interdict they propose is difficult to rationalize, but the other occurrences of $d\bar{a}t$ refer to the law of the Medes and Persians (vv. 8, 12, and 15), which threatens to send Daniel to his death. Daniel is given no opportunity to say it, as this story is told, but the issue is clear to every reader: Whose law must he obey—the law of the Medes and Persians or the law of the living God (vv. 20 and 26)?

Exegetical Analysis

Daniel the Administrator (6:1-3)

According to the inscriptions of Darius I, he organized the Persian empire into twenty-one (later twenty-three, then twenty-nine) satrapies. Each of the satrapies was divided into smaller provinces, so if the number one hundred twenty in verse 1 has any validity, it may approximate the total number of administrative units. Note that in verse 7 other officials, in addition to satraps, are listed. There is no evidence for the existence of three "presidents" in the system of Darius I. How Daniel is supposed to have moved from chief of the diviners under Belshazzar to one of the three highest officials in the Persian (Median?) empire is not explained, but we are told that his superior qualities (for "excellent spirit," compare "spirit of the holy gods" in 4:9; 5:11, 14) soon lead Darius to plan to make him prime minister.

The Conspiracy (6:4-9)

The reaction to Daniel's proposed promotion is not surprising, for the same envy and resultant plotting has occurred again and again in government and in business. The key word that appears immediately, *bᶜh* ("seek, request"), which will lie at the heart of the interdict, is translated here by the New Revised Standard Version as "tried to find." The investigators find nothing, however, and someone, knowing Daniel's practice of praying where he can be seen, three times a day, thinks of a new law *(dāt)* that would be likely to entrap him. They assume he will continue to be faithful to the law *(dāt)* of his God. Some translators prefer "his religion" at this point, but this disguises from the reader the tension between the two laws.

Why they would have proposed just this law, and why Darius would have taken it seriously enough to approve it remains a mystery. As Montgomery says, it is easier to believe Daniel escaped the lions than to believe such a law was ever passed (Montgomery 1927, 268). If the story was originally told about Darius I, the edict is not explainable, for he depicted himself as a good Zoroastrian. It seems doubtful that he would have forbidden everyone in the empire (Zoroastrians included) to pray, and he would not have claimed to take the place of God. But our author speaks of some unknown king, and perhaps was attributing a measure of *hybris* to him, as he did in chapter 4. Why no petitions to any person or god for only thirty days, however? Perhaps just long enough to catch Daniel, the only real point of the law. And was it really true that the laws of the Medes and Persians could not be changed? The answer is certainly no. Ezra 4:21 speaks of a royal order from Artaxerxes that he states he may countermand later, and there is no evidence in history that any oriental potentate accepted that sort of restriction on his power. But the concept is necessary for this story, since the friendship of the king for Daniel is an important part of it. So the reader must accept some narrative devices: a law that no one can revoke, and a king who could be persuaded to approve such a strange interdict.

Daniel Resists (6:10-15)

Daniel knows about the new law, so what he proceeds to do is deliberate. He does not set out to look for trouble, for he simply continues to do what has always been his practice. He is not commanded by Jewish law to pray three times a day, so he can easily find an excuse that might not violate his conscience; but this new law seeks to tell him how he *cannot* worship his God. That creates the issue for him that will be developed further in the theological and ethical analysis.

His form of prayer has been of great interest to readers. Prayer both standing (Neh 9:5) and kneeling (Ezra 9:5) is mentioned in Scripture. Prayer "evening and morning and at noon" is mentioned in Ps 55:17, but the usual custom was to pray at the times of the morning and afternoon sacrifices in the Temple (1 Chron 23:30). First Kings 8:48 already speaks of prayers of exiles facing Jerusalem, and Tob 3:10-11 contains a close parallel to Daniel's practice of prayer in an upper room, facing a window. For Daniel, the open windows mean he makes no effort to hide what he is doing, and his violation of the interdict is evident to all.

The case is more straightforward than in chapter 3. The three young men neglect to do something which the king gives them an opportunity to remedy by agreeing to obey next time. They use it as an opportunity to testify to what they believe, instead. Daniel has done something that was forbidden; there was no undoing that, and the act itself was his testimony that he would accept no restrictions on the practice of his religion. All the conspirators needed to do, then, was remind the king of the law he had approved, and Daniel stood condemned (vv. 12-13). Now we learn how important Daniel is to the king, for the king was greatly distressed when he learned the effects of the law and spent the rest of the day looking for a loophole. But, contrary to what would have been possible for a real emperor, he is helpless before the law of the Medes and the Persians that cannot be changed, and must agree to the insistence of the conspirators (vv. 15-16).

The Lion Pit (6:16-24)

The king could not save him, so all this mighty emperor can do is to express his hope that Daniel's God will do so. Two words for "save" or "rescue" had been used of his efforts in verse 14, one of them reappears in verses 16 and 20, and both again in verse 27, and in each of the last three occasions God is the subject. The king moves from his own futile efforts to save, to a hope concerning Daniel's God, and finally to a certainty that in fact this God is able to save. But in the meantime, the pit (the literal translation of the word) is covered with a stone and sealed by the king and other officials, so that neither friend nor enemy can tamper with it. Lions were captured and kept in cages by oriental kings, but there is no evidence they did, or could keep them in such a pit. This is not the most unrealistic part of the story, however.

The king is not as wise as he might have been, but except for that he is depicted in an entirely positive way. Unlike Nebuchadnezzar, who was enraged when his decree was violated (3:13, 19), Darius becomes angry only because the new law has trapped his friend. He tries everything to avoid condemning him, and now spends a sleepless night, presumably of mixed guilt and grief. The picture of a basically good man is continued with him arising at dawn, hurrying to the pit, and even crying out to Daniel, whom he hopes might still be alive. His choice of words is remarkable: "Servant of the living God." As king, he could condemn to death; was there a God of life with power even over death itself? Daniel's polite answer contains a bit of irony in this · setting: "O king, live forever!" And he affirms his essential innocence (v. 22). He had engaged in "civil disobedience," but he had done the king and the empire no *harm* (a better translation than "I have done no wrong").

Those who had conspired against Daniel then suffered the fate they had desired for him, along with their wives and children. This kind of rough justice troubles readers, but there is no need to try to account for this in terms of the Old Testament ethos (corporate responsibility, as in Josh 7:24-26; or punishment for false witnesses, as in Deut 19:18-19). This is a Persian (Median?) king, and Persian executions notoriously took severe forms.

The Proclamation (6:25-28)

Darius's encyclical letter begins with the same words as Nebuchadnezzar's (3:29; 4:1) and praises Daniel's God with similar language, but he goes beyond Nebuchadnezzar, who threatened severe punishment for anyone who spoke against God (3:29). Darius's decree seems to call for a positive acknowledgment of Daniel's God, for all peoples, nations, and languages are to "tremble and fear" before him. Commentators note the irony. One law had tried to suppress, temporarily, one form of religious practice. An unexpected result of that law is another one, now intending to make sure that one religion is acknowledged by everyone. Many a subsequent religious ordinance, positive or negative, has echoed the futile legislative efforts recounted in this chapter.

Theological and Ethical Analysis

The king who is Daniel's friend reminds us of a kind of pressure to compromise with what we believe and how we should behave that is more insidious and more common than the overt demand made by Nebuchadnezzar with his order to bow down to a golden image. Nebuchadnezzar plays the role of the enemy, and it can be hard enough to summon the courage to resist an enemy, but enemies and resistance go together. Something more than courage is involved when the pressure to compromise comes from a friend, for those issues are hard not only on oneself but also on the friend. The storyteller makes that very clear with the attention he gives to

Darius's distress. He attributes no emotion to Daniel, so we are allowed, if we insist, to see him as an unfeeling fanatic, not caring how his behavior affects Darius; however, the story loses some of its power then. If we imagine Daniel wishing he did not have to put his beneficent employer into the position of having to pronounce the death sentence—even embarrassed by the necessity his conscience placed upon him—we can appreciate how difficult ethical decisions can sometimes be in a friendly environment. Why not find some way to avoid creating a crisis, even if the compromise bothers the conscience? The story itself raises that question, for Daniel could have found a way out.

The situation created for the intent of this story would have allowed Daniel not to create an issue, and in this his situation is also different from the one that faced the friends in chapter 3. The edict was a temporary one, for thirty days, and what would have been so wrong with refraining from prayer for thirty days? Or, he might have continued praying in private rather than before the open window where everyone could see. Neither of these options would have been a serious violation of his religious principles— nothing like bowing before an idol. But this leads us to the heart of the issue the story sets before us. Daniel could not let it *appear* that the law of the state took precedence over the law of his God. Never mind that to interrupt his prayer life would not even violate any specific Jewish law. The issue for Daniel was this: To whom do I owe my fundamental, primary loyalty? He saw the interdict as a claim that loyalty to the state (the king) takes precedence over every other loyalty, and he understood that even to *appear* to obey was to accept that claim.

We have an expression for what is involved here: freedom of the conscience. The author knew of no such term and was ahead of his time in thinking this way, but he understood the concept.

DANIEL 7

Everything changes in this chapter except the language, which is still Aramaic. Daniel himself becomes the narrator from verse 2 on, and there are no more stories of life in royal courts. Most of what follows is a report of Daniel's visionary experiences. There are parallels with Nebuchadnezzar's dream in chapter 2, but the parallels serve to emphasize the differences in setting and outlook between the two chapters.

The fact that chapter 7 agrees in language with chapters 2–6 and in genre with 8–12, plus the use of chapter 2's four-kingdom pattern to convey a message like that of chapters 8, 9, and 11, have led commentators to call this chapter the center or hinge-point of the book. Its style and its message agree entirely with the second half of the book, however. The attitude toward the nations is new; no longer do they offer a potential for a successful life, for their only quality that is described is destructiveness. The Jewish people are not mentioned in chapter 2, but it is their suffering and the promise to them of victory that is the major theme of chapter 7. The basically reasonable kings of chapters 1–6 have disappeared, and now we encounter the archtyrant whose death is the only basis for hope.

Chapter 7 has attracted a great deal of attention from scholars, not so much for its own sake as for its potential contribution to the effort to understand the uses of the term "Son of Man" in the New Testament. In this brief commentary, there is no room for discussion of "Son of Man" in the literature later than Daniel. Neither is there room to cite all the theories concerning possible mythological origins of various concepts in the chapter. Most of them contribute little, if anything, to our understanding of its message. Hence we shall attempt to determine what the author of the chapter explicitly takes to be meaningful in the symbolism he uses, and focus on that. The parallels are interesting, and the various theories can be found discussed in the larger commentaries, but within these limits what is merely interesting must be left to one side in order to focus on what seems important to the author.

Literary Analysis

The outline of this chapter is a bit more complex than that of the others in the book, and some apparent interruptions of continuity have led earlier commentators to suggest at least two separate stages of composition. Recent commentaries tend to read the chapter as a unit, and that will be done here. After a one-verse introduction in the third person, Daniel recounts his vision in what may be called four scenes: the four beasts (vv. 2-8), the Ancient One (vv. 9-10), the destruction of the fourth beast (vv. 11-12), and the "one like a human being" (vv. 13-14). His reaction and desire for an explanation follow (vv. 15-16). Two aspects of the complex vision are chosen for interpretation: the four beasts and the gift of the kingdom (vv. 17-18; note that the humanlike figure is not mentioned here). Daniel then asks for an additional explanation of the fourth beast, now adding considerable detail concerning what he had seen (vv. 19-22). The interpretation that follows deals with the beast, its ten horns, the little horn, and once again the gift of the kingdom (vv. 23-27). Daniel's reaction to it all concludes the chapter (v. 28).

This is a symbolic dream vision with a brief historical introduction. It contains several of the characteristics that are typical of apocalyptic literature. The history that interests the author is divided into four periods, with the last one leading to the triumph of God over the forces of evil as represented by the nations of the world. This schematization of history does not appear elsewhere in the Old Testament except in Dan 2, but reappears in various forms in *Assumption of Moses 2–10, 1 Enoch 83–90, Testament of Abraham, Apocalypse of Abraham 23–31, 2 Baruch 53–74.* The vision involves a variety of symbolic elements, several of which, such as colors and numbers, became standard "codes" in apocalyptic literature. In this chapter the animals, the horns, the color white, and the numbers ten and three are elements that are reused by other apocalyptic writers (e.g., Rev 13). There are parallels to this symbolism elsewhere in the Old Testament, but in apocalyptic literature the symbols are considered to be cryptic until they are explained by a supernatural figure, as in Dan 7:16 (note also 8:15-17; Rev 7:14; 17:7). The role of the heavenly interpreter first appears in the visions of Zechariah (1:9, 19; 4:4). The visions typically have profound physical effects on the seer, and there are elements of that in verses 15 and 28. They are more extreme in 8:18 and 10:8-9, 17. Ezekiel was affected in similar ways (Ezek 1:28*b*; 3:15*b*). His visions and those of Zechariah are certainly the predecessors of those experienced by Daniel, but chapters 7–12 of this book are the only parts of the Old Testament that fit the generally accepted way of describing apocalyptic literature (Collins 1979, 1-19).

The originality of this chapter, when compared with the rest of the Old Testament, has led to an extensive search through the literature and iconography of the ancient Near East for possible sources of the ideas and imagery that appear here. The monstrous, composite beasts, and the humanlike figure coming with clouds of heaven have no clear parallels in the Old Testament. The result of a century or more of searching is a group of theories which, examined critically, have actually contributed little to our understanding of the meaning of the chapter, even if any of them could be demonstrated to be an actual source used by the author. Many of the commentators who evaluate the theories at length finally acknowledge the great originality of this author, admitting that if traditional elements have been used, they are used in a distinctive way, with earlier meanings contributing little if anything to the point of the present text.

Originally, Babylonian and Iranian sources were considered, but the Ugaritic texts, discovered in Syria in 1929, contain closer parallels. They speak of an older and a younger god—with El, called "father of years"; and Baal, "rider on the clouds"—doing battle with the sea god Yam. This has suggested to many that Daniel made use of Canaanite mythology, even though the Ugaritic texts are about one thousand years earlier than Daniel. (For a full discussion, see Collins 1993, 280-94.)

The differences between Daniel 7 and the Ugaritic texts are as important as the similarities. In brief, much has been made of the reference to the sea as the source of the beasts (7:2), calling it an echo of the use of the sea as a chaotic power in Babylonian and Ugaritic myth; but the author of Dan 7 makes nothing of the sea. The beasts are not aquatic animals (they resemble lion, bear, and leopard), and the introduction by modern interpreters of references to creation has no basis in the author's interpretation of the vision. The myths all involve combat, which is missing from this chapter. The fourth beast is simply killed and burned, with no reference to any agent. Extensive searches have uncovered nothing that can properly be called a "Son of Man" tradition earlier than this chapter (Casey 1979, 48). The reader is referred to the larger commentaries for full discussion of the efforts to discover traditions that might account for various details in the vision.

The most dramatic difference between this vision and the dream in chapter 2 is the appearance of the "little horn," the archtyrant who played no role in the earlier chapter. As described in 7:25 he is clearly Antiochus IV Epiphanes (175–164 BC), and his "attempt to change the sacred seasons and the law," without any mention of his desecration of the Temple (as in 8:11-13; 9:27; and 11:31), suggests that this chapter was written shortly after his decree proscribing the practice of Judaism, late in 167. Since it is in Aramaic, it seems likely that it was added to an earlier collection of stories, chapters 2–6, at that time. It was certainly written in Judea with the intent of providing encouragement for the faithful Jews who were already beginning to suffer for their religion (vv. 21 and 25).

Exegetical Analysis

The Vision (7:1-14)

The second half of the book is associated with the earlier chapters by a series of dates, which locate the visions during the reigns of Belshazzar, Darius, and Cyrus. The expression "dream and visions of his head" (v. 1) provides a link with chapters 2 and 4 (cf. 4:5), but now it is Daniel who experiences dream and vision, and needs another to interpret it for him. The writing of the dream becomes an important element for apocalyptic literature, since often apocalyptic literature is said to reveal something that will be completely understood only at a later time (12:4, 9; contrast Rev 22:10).

The sea from which the beasts come certainly is depicted as a chaotic, threatening place elsewhere in the Old Testament (Gen 1:2; Job 26:12-13; Pss 74:13-14; 89:9-10; Isa 27:1; 51:9-10), and the brief reference to the sea and the four winds in verse 2 has led some commentators to take it as a key to the cosmic (mythological) substratum of the text. In fact, the author makes nothing of sea and winds, and even interprets the beasts as kings from the *earth* in verse 17. This appears to be a detail of no great importance to the meaning of the vision.

The beasts that appear are not sea monsters, so there is no significant parallel with the *tannin* (dragon) in Ezek 29 and 32, or Rahab or Leviathan in the texts noted above. Herculean efforts to find predecessors for the first three composite creatures have failed, and many commentators now admit that they must be the products of the author's own mind (or visionary experience). Composite beasts of various kinds were commonplace in ancient Near Eastern art, and this could have been enough to produce the mental images Daniel describes. The description of the lionlike creature rather clearly makes it a representation of Babylon (cf. v. 4 with 4:34), and the identification of the little horn with Antiochus IV Epiphanes means the fourth beast is to be identified with the hellenistic era. Horns were standard symbols for power (Ps 75:4, 5, 10) and thus for kingship (Pss 89:24; 132:17). Many different lists of kings have been proposed for the ten and the three, but the author offers no clues to their identity except that they lead up to the appearance of the little horn (for the lists, see Caragounis 1987).

The first three beasts looked in part like known animals, but the fourth is incomparable. It can be described only as having iron teeth and being different from the others (v. 7). It is called different probably because its origin is Greece; it represents a European rather than an Asiatic empire. The most that can be said of it refers to its destructive activity. Its ten horns seem to serve as a quick summary of the Seleucid dynasty, recounted with more care in chapter 11; and the three that were plucked up may represent Seleucus IV and his sons Antiochus and Demetrius, whose claims to the throne were prior to that of Antiochus IV Epiphanes, but there is no agreement on that. The author must have assumed his original readers could identify them, but they are important only as predecessors to the little horn.

A new scene is introduced by "as I watched" (vv. 9-10). We are given no hint of its location, but most interpreters assume the seer now views what goes on in heaven. Or, are we to think the thrones are set in the immediate presence of the beasts? The imagery makes it clear that it is God who takes his throne in order to pronounce judgment, but, as is characteristic of apocalyptic style, he is not called God or the Most High, as elsewhere in the book. Everything is alluded to in mysterious language, so here he is called Ancient of Days ("Ancient One" in the New Revised Standard Version). The whiteness of his clothing and hair may represent purity, or may be a part of the blinding brilliance of the whole scene (Goldingay 1989, 165). The fire is a regular feature of theophanies (e.g., Exod 19; Ps 18:8, 12; Ezek 1), representing an awe-inspiring supernatural force, and important also for its brightness. The throne with wheels is reminiscent of Ezekiel's vision in 1:15-21. The other rarely occurring visions of God in the Old Testament also involve a court scene with attendants around the divine throne (1 Kgs 22:19-22; Job 1; Isa 6). So all of this is familiar except for the title used of God. As we read on, it becomes clear that the opened books are records that become the basis for judgment (see Isa 65:6-7), although the author is not explicit about that. No trial is described and no judgment is pronounced.

Daniel is still in the presence of the little horn, for he alludes again in verse 11 to its arrogant speech. The continuity between verses 8 and 11 has led some scholars to propose that verses 9-10 had been inserted into the original vision account, but that would have left the destruction of the beast without any explanation. The court scene is needed where it stands. Only the fourth beast is destroyed in this vision, unlike the dream of chapter 2 in which the entire statue disappeared. The other three are allowed to live, but with their power taken away. Rowley and others have suggested this expresses a hope that the Asiatic nations may regain their freedom from hellenistic domination, but without the power to tyrannize other peoples as in the past (Rowley 1935, 123).

Now there appears before the Ancient One a new figure, *kĕbar ᵓĕnāš* (literally, "one like a son of a man"), a common Semitic idiom meaning one like a human being, or simply, "someone." As the beasts were *like* a lion, similar to a bear, and *like* a leopard, this is a humanlike figure. As the beasts will be interpreted as symbols of kings (v. 17), so also the humanlike figure will be replaced in the explanation by the "holy ones of the Most High," which the figure symbolizes (vv. 18, 21, and 27). One of the great debates concerning verses 13-14 deals with the question of whether the humanlike figure is supposed to have any identity in himself; that is, to be more than just a symbol for the historical reality, the holy ones. There would have been no proliferation of literature on the subject if the term "Son of Man" had not been used with such prominence in the Gospels, with some of those references clearly echoing Daniel (e.g., Matt 26:64). For E. J. Young the Gospels settle the matter; Christ is the Son of Man who appeared to Daniel (Young 1949, 154-56, 293-94; Miller 1994, 207-10). John Collins offers an able defense of the theory that Michael, who is named in Dan 10:13, 21 as Israel's guardian angel, is the figure who appeared with the clouds in 7:13 (Collins 1993, 304-10). Other theories claiming the figure is a remnant of one mythological character or another involve parallels so remote as to be very doubtful. (For a list of attempted identifications, see Redditt 1999, 126-27.) The identity of the figure, if it had an identity other than symbolic, seems unimportant to Daniel, however. He does not ask for an interpretation, the term "Son of Man" occurs only once and is replaced immediately by "holy ones of the Most High," and the eternal dominion given to the humanlike figure in the vision is a dominion that in reality will be given to those holy ones. For Dan 7 (not for the subsequent use of the term), then, the term "Son of Man" does not seem to be as important as the identity of the holy ones. (For defense of the position taken here, that the humanlike figure is only symbolic, see Montgomery 1927, 317-23; Di Lella 1977; Casey 1979, 7-48; Goldingay 1989, 169-70.) The language of verse 14 is strongly reminiscent of what has been said of human kingship, of divine kingship, and of the eschatological kingdom in the earlier chapters. Nebuchadnezzar is said to have been given "the kingdom, the power, the might, and the glory" (2:37) over "all peoples, nations, and languages" (5:19), so this language can be used of human rule, a detail that is important for interpreting verses 18, 21, and

27. Nebuchadnezzar's kingdom is not said to be everlasting, however. That distinction is reserved for the kingdom of the Most High (4:3, 34; 6:26), and in the dream of chapter 2 it is a kingdom that will never be destroyed that will take the place of all earthly kingdoms (2:44). That is the kingdom promised here.

Daniel's Reaction and the Initial Interpretation (7:15-18)

Daniel is affected by the vision as Nebuchadnezzar had been affected by his dreams. Daniel is afraid and does not understand what the vision means but is still in the visionary state, for now he asks one of the multitude surrounding the throne to explain it. This sort of procedure first appeared in Zech 1–6 and became a familiar feature in apocalyptic literature from this time on. The answer is given immediately and briefly, and is valuable for its identification of what the author considered to be important among the things Daniel saw.

The little horn is ignored at first because much more needs to be said about it. The symbolism of the beasts is explained in the briefest possible way, for they are not a central concern of the author. They represent four kings, and in this context king can represent kingdom. Only one other feature is chosen for interpretation, and that is the identity of the recipients of the eternal kingdom as the holy ones of the Most High. Daniel must assume the reader will know who these holy ones are, for no further identification is offered; yet for later interpreters this allusion has created a challenge, which will be taken up here in association with verse 27. Thus the one feature of this elaborate vision initially chosen for emphasis is the promise with which it concluded.

Additional Details from the Vision (7:19-22)

The promise as originally offered in verse 18 is too bland, for it is addressed to people who may be facing death because of their religion. Is that little horn Antiochus IV Epiphanes, the one who is just now attacking their way of life and what they believe? That needs to be made clear; so Daniel offers additional information about the little horn that had not been included in his original description, and still more is added in the elaborate interpretation that follows. The important new piece of information appears in verse 21: "this horn made war with the holy ones and was prevailing over them." The holy ones have been identified with the humanlike figure in verse 17, since they receive the kingdom, but the author has now partly dropped symbolic language, since "one like a son of man" does not reappear. "The holy ones" must refer to the real world, while the horn remains the symbol for their enemy. We now learn that the most important aspect of the terribly destructive behavior of the fourth beast is the temporarily successful attack of the little horn on the holy ones. Who they are, whether angels or the faithful members of the Jewish people, continues to be discussed by scholars (see v. 27). All the other details of the vision (including the "Son of Man") fade into the background as what really matters is emphasized: a clear identification of the little horn and a reassurance of victory over him for the holy ones.

The Full Explanation (7:23-28)

The heavenly interpreter now adds more detail concerning the actions of the little horn. Once again the fourth beast is identified as a kingdom different from the others (vv. 7 and 22), a likely reference to the impact of hellenistic culture on the Near East after Alexander's conquests. Nothing new is said about the ten kings and three kings, for they have no effect on the future of the holy ones (vv. 7-8, 20, and 24). The little horn's arrogant speech is now called "words against the Most High" (vv. 8, 20, and 25). His attack on the holy ones is said to be an affront against God himself. There are important parallels to verse 25 in Dan 8:9-14, 23-25 and 11:36-37. All scholars, including the most conservative, agree that the little horn in chapter 8 is Antiochus IV Epiphanes. Part of what is said of him there is literal; he brought an end to the regular burnt offering in the Jerusalem temple, occupied it and used it for offerings to Zeus (8:11-13). But this is mingled with theological language. He "grew as high as the host of heaven" (cf. Isa 14:13-14), "threw down to the earth some of the host and some of the stars, and trampled on them," and "cast truth to the ground" (8:10, 12). The accusation appears in more literal terms in 11:36: "He shall exalt himself and consider himself greater than any god." This accusation is based on two facts concerning Antiochus. In calling himself Epiphanes he did claim to be an epiphany, an appearance of god on earth. His persecution of the Jews was probably not associated with that, but was for political reasons. Daniel, however, does not make such a distinction. The decision to bring the worship of Yahweh to an end was seen as an effort to attack Yahweh himself, and that understanding was supported by Antiochus's personal claims. The extravagant language of 8:10 makes him attack even the stars. Some scholars take that as a parallel to "wear out the holy ones of the Most High" in 7:25 and use it as evidence that the holy ones are angels (Collins 1993, 320). Others think the verb "wear out" more appropriately speaks of the suffering of the Jews, especially since the next clause explicitly refers to what was done to them, not to angels. "[He] shall attempt to change the sacred seasons and the law" refers to the decree of 167 BC forbidding Jews to practice their religion, the effects of which are described in detail in 1 Macc 1:44-61 and 2 Macc 6–7.

Now the interpreter of the vision not only promises eventual victory over the tyrant but sets a time limit on his successes: "They shall be given into his power for a time, times, and half a time." This is typical of apocalyptic style, using allusive language rather than saying things literally, and it leaves commentators with the options of an indefinite (Goldingay 1989, 181) or a definite period; that is, three and one-half years (Montgomery 1927, 312-14, and most others). The parallels with the numbers in 8:14 and 9:27 support understanding it as three and one-half years, and thus very likely as evidence this chapter was written before the persecution ended, since, according to 1 Macc 4:54, it lasted three years (only two years according to 2 Macc 10:3).

The vision concludes with a reaffirmation and elaboration of the promise. The court, sitting in judgment, is responsible for bringing the dominion of the little horn to an end (cf. v. 11), and the description of the eternal kingdom that is to come uses the same language as verse 14 but expands it at even greater length. In the vision it was given to the one like a Son of Man, who was then identified with the holy ones of the Most High in verses 18 and 22, and now the recipients are called the people of the holy ones of the Most High. An article by Martin Noth has been responsible for serious consideration of the suggestion that these expressions refer to angels, not to the faithful Jews (Noth 1966a, 215-28). The idea has not been widely accepted, but Collins has corrected some of the weaknesses of Noth's argument and has made a strong case for the angelic reference (Collins 1993, 312-17). In the Old Testament, Apocrypha, Pseudepigrapha, and Dead Sea Scrolls both angels and human beings may be called "holy ones," so the usage elsewhere does not settle the question (Brekelmans 1965, 305-29). In Dan 4:13, 17, 23; 8:13 the term refers to angels, but 12:7 speaks of a holy people. The decision must be based on the way the term is used in chapter 7. Collins argues, from the use of animals to represent people and human figures to represent angels in the *Animal Apocalypse* of Enoch, that the same pattern appears here (*1 Enoch* 85–90). The beasts represent kings; the one like a human being must then represent angels, here called the holy ones. The writers of apocalyptic literature tended to be highly individualistic in their use of symbolism, however, and it is risky to assume that any two authors used imagery in exactly the same way. Collins does agree that in verse 27 "the *people* of the holy ones of the Most High" are the faithful Jews, and cites texts in the *War Scroll* from Qumran (1QM 10:10; 12:1-7; 17:7-8) to support his conclusion that Dan 7 speaks of the kingdom being given both to angels and humans (Collins 1993, 318-19). He thus reads "people of" as a possessive genitive, that is, "the people who belong to the holy ones (angels)." Those who believe the holy ones are humans read it as epexegetical: "the people who are the holy ones." As the debate has progressed, it begins to appear that the identity of the "holy ones" is less crucial than it had seemed, for both Collins and those who argue against the angelic theory agree that the faithful Jews are to be the recipients of the everlasting kingdom.

The chapter concludes with another of the typical descriptions of the intense physical effects of a visionary experience that are characteristic of this kind of literature.

Theological and Ethical Analysis

The text of this chapter strongly emphasizes visionary elements. The verb for seeing occurs fifteen times in various forms. In spite of this emphasis on what Daniel saw, however, the means of revelation in the chapter is still the spoken word. Daniel himself does not claim to understand the meaning of anything he saw, and this is a typical feature of many vision-accounts. In earlier reports of visions, God immediately provides explanations (see Amos 7–8); in apocalyptic literature from Daniel on, the seer asks and an interpreter answers. Accurate communication is essential, and visual symbols remain indeterminate apart from words. (For example, the bread and the cup at a communion service might be taken to represent all sorts of things by one who knows nothing of the *text* that gives the bread and cup meaning for the worshipers. No one would connect the items with a death on a cross without that text.) What is seen in the visions remains meaningless until words explain it. Language is the sole means of revelation in Scripture. Why the pictures, then, if they provide only the occasion for words? The initial explanation is probably that some people do experience dreams and visions of this kind, and in a few cases in the past the interpretation of the images that were seen had such an impact that they were preserved and became part of Holy Scripture. For some reason less easily explainable, accounts of visions came to be favored by the writers of apocalyptic literature, whether or not each of the accounts was really based on a personal experience.

If Dan 2 was written before the time of Antiochus IV Epiphanes, as it seems to have been, the succession of four empires represented by the statue already is evidence for new theological reflections on the meaning of history within Judaism. The Prophets had interpreted the wars of the empire-builders—Assyria, Babylonia, and Persia—in turn as evidence of Yahweh's intervention in human history in order to accomplish his will for his own people, Israel. Those messages had direct relevance for the times when they were uttered, but in 538 BC an old person might have lived during the rule of all three of those empires (Nineveh fell in 612, seventy-three years before the Persians occupied Babylon in 539). The changes in world history during one lifetime may have led to reflection on what this meant in the light of the prophetic insistence that Yahweh was in control of history and was moving it toward blessing for Israel and the world (see Noth 1966b, 201). Then came the Greeks, and the consummation was no nearer; to be a Jew anywhere in the world meant to live under pagan rule. The stories in Daniel claimed that could be done successfully, but Nebuchadnezzar's dream again took up the old message. The succession of empires will not go on forever; the kingdom of God will come, and the hellenistic kingdoms will be the last of the sequence.

In 167 BC when to be a practicing Jew meant that one might die under torture, that message became more than a philosophy of history. The vision in chapter 7 sees the succession of empires as a history no longer of God's work, but of evil powers, for the empires are symbolized not as valuable metals, but as destructive monsters. The fourth empire is more evil than its predecessors, and the one king of importance is an archtyrant, no agent of God's will (as in the Prophets), but the enemy of God and God's people. Divine intervention now becomes an immediate necessity, not just something to be hoped for "in that day," if any people of Yahweh are to survive. So, in chapter 7 and the subsequent chapters, written in a time of persecution in order to offer hope to a suffering people, the answer to "How long?" must be that the kingdom is coming soon.

The kingdom did not come in its fullness within three and one-half years after Dan 7 was written, and for those who insist that the promises of Scripture must be fulfilled literally and exactly, this delay can be a problem. A favorite solution to the problem has been to call the fourth empire Rome so as to make the fulfillment the coming of Christ; but the kingdom did not come in its fullness in the first century AD, either. So, others introduce a leap over a long span of history and make this a promise concerning the eschaton, still awaited. In a meaningful way, the promise in this passage did come true in the second century, however, for within the three and one-half years after 167 the persecution came to an end and soon a Jewish kingdom (the Hasmonean dynasty) was established. It was not the kingdom of God, by any means;

but the sudden end of the rule of Antiochus IV Epiphanes must have contributed to the acceptance by the Jewish people of the visions of Daniel as authentic revelation.

The persecution under Antiochus produced a change in the Jewish attitude toward foreign rule which is documented clearly in the two halves of Daniel. Especially in the apocalyptic literature which succeeded this book, but not only there, the Gentile nations are associated with the powers of evil, even on a cosmic level, and history becomes the battleground between God and the forces of evil. For some Jews, this attitude led to the conviction that foreign rule was intolerable. The community that lived at Qumran from the second century BC through the first century AD produced the War Scroll, which looks forward to a great, eschatological battle in which the nations (the sons of darkness) will finally be defeated by the sons of light. In AD 66 the "zealots" among the Jews incited the people to war with Rome, considering themselves to be the heirs of the Maccabees, who had once freed the Jews from foreign domination. For many centuries the thoroughness of the Roman victory led most Jews to reject violence and to strive to find peaceful ways to live among the Gentiles. That was in keeping with the attitude of the book of Daniel, which contains no calls to violent action but finds hope only in the conviction that God will soon intervene. Apocalyptic literature is sometimes criticized for its quietism, but its dark view of history—associating those who do not believe as you do with the power of evil that must be destroyed—at times has also made it a basis for calls to violent action. Two possible kinds of resistance to evil are thus implied in this literature: faithful suffering, if need be, in the hope that faithfulness itself will triumph; or active resistance with violence, if need be, even though it brings evil into the world as it combats evil.

DANIEL 8

Literary Analysis

This chapter contains the account of another symbolic vision, following the same basic pattern as chapter 7 but with a simpler structure and less elaborate imagery. After an introduction that supplies not only date but also place (vv. 1-2), the vision is described (vv. 3-14), an interpretation is provided (vv. 15-25), and Daniel's reaction is reported (vv. 26-27). The subject is also the same as that of the preceding chapter. World empires appear again, but only to introduce the author's main concern. This chapter moves more directly and more explicitly to the crimes of Antiochus IV Epiphanes, and reaches its climax more briefly with the assurance that within a measurable time he will meet his end.

Several of the features that are typical of apocalyptic literature appear. Animals represent kingdoms, and horns stand for kings. The kingdoms are named, this time, modifying somewhat the air of mystery that is characteristic of apocalyptic literature, but no kings are named. An interpretation by a heavenly figure is offered, and the beginnings of the interest in angelology that is typical of this genre of literature may be seen. The physical and emotional effects of the experience on the seer are emphasized. The basis for the message of hope is a reassurance that the time of suffering will not last much longer, for God will soon intervene.

Without warning, the language has changed to Hebrew at this point. The style is straightforward until the activities of the little horn are described. Then, in the vision (vv. 10-12) and in the interpretation (vv. 23-25), the language becomes difficult, and translation of parts of these verses is uncertain. It is always possible that the text has been poorly transmitted, but it is probably not coincidence that the difficulty appears just at these points. We cannot be sure of the reason, but it seems appropriate that the disturbed nature of the language reflects the intensity of the crisis that concerns the seer. It may be that Daniel actually saw things he could not describe any better than this, or he may have deliberately chosen to use rather confused language because of the awfulness of the sacrilege he refers to—the profanation of the Temple itself.

Unlike the fantastic creatures in chapter 7, the male sheep (ram) and male goat (buck) of this chapter were simply part of the everyday scenery. The sheep/shepherd metaphor occurs frequently in the Old Testament to represent the relationship between Israel and God, but it has nothing in common with the way the metaphor is used here to represent empires.

The language used of the little horn's *hybris* has its roots in ancient Near Eastern myths of conflict among the gods. It probably reflects a knowledge of Isa 14:4-21, which already reused those mythical themes in order to speak of the self-deifying claims of a great king:

> You said in your heart,
>> "I will ascend to heaven;
> I will raise my throne
>> above the stars of God;
> I will sit on the mount of assembly
>> on the heights of Zaphon;
> I will ascend to the tops of the clouds,
>> I will make myself like the Most High."
>>> (Isa 14:13-14)

Here is the attempt to ascend to heaven, and the challenge to the stars (Dan 8:10), as well as the claim to rival even God himself (Dan 8:11, 25). The Mesopotamian myth of Zu spoke of a divine figure who rebelled against Enlil, king of the gods, and stole the tablets of destiny, leading to chaos until Zu was vanquished (Pritchard 1955, 111-13, Pritchard 1969, 514-17). There are Hittite and Greek myths that tell of uncontrolled, intrafamily struggles among the gods for supreme power, such as the Hittite Kumarbi and Ullikumi texts (Pritchard 1955, 120-125) and the Greek Titanomachis, known from Hesiod's *Theogony*. Contests between mortals and gods also appear in Greek myths (Gowan 1975, 50-67). Isaiah 14 uses these familiar themes as a way of accusing the great king of making claims for himself that far outreach what his power entitles him to. He cannot, of course, ascend into the heavens, but he has come too near to making himself a rival of the only God there is; so his aspirations and his inevitable fall have been compared with the myths of overly ambitious gods and mortals. Those who take this language literally insist it could not refer to anything Antiochus did, and must therefore speak of the antichrist; but that is to misunderstand the creative use the Old Testament authors could make of traditional materials.

The desecration of the temple reported in 1 Macc 1:59 and

2 Macc 5:15-15; 6:2-6 is referred to in Dan 8:11-13, and there is no indication in Dan 8 of knowledge concerning the reestablishment of the worship of Yahweh. The altar to Zeus was set up on 15 Chislev 167, and the new altar to Yahweh was consecrated on 25 Chislev 164, so Dan 8 must have been written between those two dates. Since chapter 7 knows of persecution but shows no awareness of the cessation of the daily offering, chapter 8 was probably written shortly after it.

The message of the chapter is for people in Judah, and one is inclined to think the author resided there also. He locates the vision in the Elamite city of Susa, however. Having decided this chapter was not written in the sixth century, we need to inquire why. The author knows a detail about the environs of the city, for he mentions the name of a canal, Ulai, which has been identified in that region.

Exegetical Analysis

The Introduction (8:1-2)

There is no evident significance to the date of this chapter, except that the clause "after the one that had appeared to me at first" seems intended to make a clear connection between this Hebrew account and the one in Aramaic that preceded it. Commentators have discussed whether Daniel is supposed to have traveled from Babylon to Susa at this time, or whether he sees himself there in the vision, as Ezekiel saw himself transported from Babylonia to Jerusalem in a vision (Ezek 8–11). This may tend to overlook the conclusion that Daniel is a legendary figure, and as such the author has simply placed him "in Susa" and said nothing more about him. The accurate detail concerning the name of the canal (New Revised Standard Version: "river"), Ulai, does raise the question of where the second-century author got his information about the city. In the vision he sees the buck (New Revised Standard Version: "male goat") attack the ram at the canal, suggesting another rationale for the location. This clearly represents Alexander's victory over the Persians. The decisive battles occurred at Issus, in Cilicia, and at Gaugamela, in north

Mesopotamia, after which Alexander marched virtually unopposed to Babylon and then to Susa, where much of the empire's great wealth was kept. There was no battle associated with Susa, but the fact that the Old Testament knew it to be the administrative capital of the Persian empire may supply a reason for the location of the vision there (Neh 1:1; Esth 1:2, 5).

The Vision (8:3-14)

The ram's two horns are identified explicitly as the kings of Media and Persia in verse 20. The fact that one animal represents the two kingdoms has been used to support identifying the second kingdom in chapters 2 and 7 as Medo-Persia, so that the fourth kingdom may be Rome. It may be noted that a single animal is the symbol for four hellenistic kingdoms in this chapter (vv. 8 and 22), so in each case the horns can stand for kingdoms as well as kings. Babylon is no longer in the picture in this vision (even though it is dated in Belshazzar's time), and the conquests of the Persians are disposed of quickly (v. 4) in order to get to the little horn. The impact of the exploits of Alexander the Great on the Near East is described in vivid terms, however. The speed with which his army moved is represented by having him cross the face of the whole earth without touching the ground (v. 5). The battle of Issus occurred in 333 BC, and by 323 Alexander had marched through Mesopotamia, Persia, and Afghanistan to the Indus River valley and back to Babylon. His defeat of the Persians is described at relatively great length in verses 6-7, then his death at age thirty-two in verse 8. Alexander had no heir who was able to maintain a claim to the empire, and it was eventually divided among four of his generals: Egypt and Palestine ruled by Ptolemy, Syria and Mesopotamia ruled by Seleucus, Asia Minor ruled by Antigonus (then Lysimachus), and Greece and Macedonia ruled by Philip (then Cassander). The four horns are not identified by name, as the author moves quickly to the appearance of the little horn, Antiochus IV Epiphanes. His father, Antiochus III, had wrested control of Palestine away from the Ptolemies, and the references in verse 9 to the south and east reflect Epiphanes' campaigns against first Egypt and then the Parthians. The somewhat surprising word at the end of the verse, ṣĕbî ("beautiful"), is used with ᵓereṣ ("land") to indicate Palestine in 11:16, 41.

Antiochus's decision to prohibit the practice of the Jewish religion and to replace it with a hellenistic cult is alluded to in verse 10 as an attack on heaven itself, with language echoing Isa 14:13-14, as noted above. The stars are also personified in Judg 5:20 and Job 38:7; and the host of heaven appears in a similar role in 1 Kgs 22:19. The "prince of the host" is identified by some as the high priest Onias III, and by others as an angel (cf. Josh 5:14, which uses the identical term), but most commentators see this as a reference to an attack on God himself, noting the use of "Prince of princes" in verse 25, and the statement that Antiochus considered himself "greater than any god" in 11:36. Although Daniel is still experiencing a vision, the language becomes literal in verses 11b-12. This is a clear reference to the occupation of the Jerusalem temple by Antiochus's forces in December of 167, and the replacement of the worship of Yahweh with the cult of Zeus.

Now Daniel hears two voices, a conversation between heavenly figures identified so far only as "holy ones" (vv. 13-14). One of the holy ones wants to know how long this desecration of the sanctuary and the cessation of sacrifice will last, and the other one knows: two thousand three hundred "evening morning"—literally. This figure has produced calculations without end. The first issue concerns the meaning of "evening morning." In Gen 1, "evening and morning" equals one day, and if that is the meaning here, 2,300 days are referred to. But the daily sacrifice was offered in evening and morning (see Ezra 3:3), and since its absence is a major issue here, many think "2,300" refers to the number of sacrifices, thus 1,150. That number of days brings us near to the three and one-half years referred to in 7:25, and the 1,295 and 1,335 days of 12:11-12, adding support to the second option. Exactly how 1,150 days compares with three and one-half years is not easy to determine, since some assume a 360-day year (probably only a theoretical year and never actually practiced), others a 364-day year, and since Judaism used a lunar calendar the length of specific years would have varied slightly from one another. In spite of a long tradition of efforts to connect this number with specific dates, then, calculations should probably be avoided. This advice applies also to another use of the number 2,300, the "year-day" principle, assuming the restoration in verse 14 refers to the eschaton. That assumption has led people to think that if one can only determine the right starting point, adding "2,300" to that year will tell one when to expect *the end*. The most famous example of such a procedure was the calculation of William Miller, who began with 457 BC (from Neh 2:1) and announced that the end would come in 1843. He attracted many followers, and, when nothing happened that year, revised his date to 1844. The disappointment that produced led to a temporary end to date-setting, but to this day the number is used by some who think there is a mystery here that they can solve. If one accepts 1,150 days as the intended time span, the mystery disappears. It is less than three and one-half years, appropriate since this vision occurred later than the one in chapter 7, and the promise of restoration of worship in the Temple did come true within that period.

The Interpretation (8:15-25)

The interpretation has a long introduction (vv. 15-19) featuring dialogue between two heavenly beings, with emphasis on Daniel's reaction to the vision. Failure of the seer to understand the meaning of what he has seen provides a way to make that meaning explicit to the reader through the words of a heavenly interpreter (vv. 15-16). In this book we find the beginnings of a developing angelology. Angels (literally "messengers") appear from time to time in Old Testament narrative but have no names or assigned roles, as they do in Intertestamental and later literature. The name of an angel appears here for the first time in the Old Testament, and Gabriel (8:16; 9:21) is joined by Michael in 10:13, 21; 12:1. *First Enoch* 1–36, which may be roughly contemporary with Dan 7–12, already has a much more developed angelology, listing the names of the seven archangels, including Gabriel and Michael, in chapter 20. Elsewhere in the Old Testament when any description of an angel is provided, the angel looks like a man. The same is true here.

The point of the visions is to explain what will come of this time of persecution, so one of the heavenly figures asks, How long? (v. 13), and Gabriel tells Daniel that the vision is for the time of the end (vv. 17 and 19). The temptation to make this vision a reference to the end of the world should be resisted. The word *qēṣ* is not yet a technical term for the eschaton. The conclusion of the chapter clearly indicates that the concern is for the end of the tyrant's work. The use of the word *zaʿam* ("wrath") in verse 19 has led to considerable discussion, since elsewhere in the Old Testament, except in Hos 7:16, it is always used to express the wrath of God against sinners, but the visions of Daniel do not claim faithful Jews are being punished for their sins. Context requires the word to refer to the wrath of the tyrant here.

The intensity of Daniel's reaction to this experience is emphasized by the use of the root *rdm*, which elsewhere denotes Adam's condition as Eve is removed from his side (Gen 2:21), the trances of Abraham and Eliphaz (Gen 15:12; Job 4:13), and the ability of Jonah to sleep through the storm at sea (Jon 1:5-6).

The interpretation begins with the proper names Media, Persia, and Greece, the only time in the book that explicit identifications are provided for symbolic language except for associating the head of gold with Nebuchadnezzar in 2:37 (although Persia and Greece are spoken of apart from symbolism in 10:20; 11:2). From verse 20 on no symbolic language is used, but personal names are still avoided. As in verses 11-12, when attention turns to the little horn the language becomes difficult. The little horn is described as insolent and understanding riddles, showing awareness of Antiochus's often puzzling behavior recorded by ancient historians (Polybius, *History* xxvi 1, 1-14). His power and depredations are described in verses 24-25, and his victims are denoted by three terms: "the mighty," "the people of the holy ones," and "the many." These terms must all designate the faithful Jews now suffering under Antiochus. His fourth would-be victim is the prince of princes, however, and that leads to an abrupt conclusion, three words in Hebrew: "without hand he-shall-be-broken." Two characteristics of Daniel's message concerning the future appear here. He sees nothing humans can do to overthrow the tyrant, but he is sure it will happen by divine intervention. He does not speculate about details of the blessed future, even though prophetic eschatology would have provided the basis for doing that. He goes no further than the general promise of an eternal kingdom, except at the end of the book, where resurrection is promised (12:2). That distinguishes Daniel from many apocalyptic works that elaborate on heaven and hell, providing detailed (but conflicting) pictures of the future of humanity after Judgment Day (cf. Rev 21–22). The author of Daniel was probably wise to show such restraint.

The Conclusion (8:26-27)

Since most apocalyptic books claimed to have been written long ago, even though they had appeared only recently, the theme of secrecy is used to account for this, as in verse 26: "Seal up the vision, for it refers to many days from now." The book of Revelation takes a different course probably because it is ascribed to a contemporary, John, and so it contains the command not to seal up the words of the book—"for the time is near" (Rev 22:10). Daniel, who had been able to explain dreams and visions previously, does not understand this one even after it has been interpreted, a part of the apocalyptic emphasis on mystery—it is only to be understood in the latter days when these things come true.

Theological and Ethical Analysis

This chapter shows less interest in the succession of empires than chapters 2 and 7 did, and chapter 11 will show even less. The earlier chapters displayed a concern for the meaning of great political power able to dominate large portions of the world, and they reaffirmed Israel's belief in the primary sovereignty of God by promising ultimate sovereignty: an eternal kingdom not made by human hands. The intensity of suffering that lies behind chapters 8–12 has narrowed the focus of concern, however, and now the symbols for Persian and Greek rule are used only to make evident the identity of the little horn. The emphasis is on assuring suffering people that his actions oppose God himself, perhaps countering claims of the hellenizing party in Jerusalem who would have been defending their compromises with traditional Judaism up to this point.

We do not know whether the Maccabean revolt had begun when this chapter was written (see 1 Macc 2:39-48; 3:1-2; 2 Macc 5:27; 8:1-5). If there had been little or no military resistance to Antiochus's decree, then the message of this chapter would have been addressed to those with no hope of physical deliverance if they insisted on practicing their religion. They would potentially face a martyr's death, like those described in 2 Macc 6 and 7. For them, the promise "he shall be broken" (8:25) would not necessarily mean being saved from a terrible death, but it would mean they would not die in vain. The martyr stories in 2 Maccabees claim that is in fact a meaningful promise. If, however, violent resistance had begun, the words "not by human hands" may indicate a deliberate choice of pacifism in the belief that if deliverance comes, it will not be by human violence but only by an act of God (cf. Dan 11:34). Lying just below the surface of these few words, then, are some major ethical issues that face people who live and die under tyranny. Apocalyptic literature was typically a message for those with little physical power, calling on them to remain faithful because they could depend on spiritual power. Many of the faithful have died in the process, but history has provided an abundance of examples that the belief in spiritual power is not nonsense.

The tendency of apocalyptic literature to assure its readers that the end is near has been regularly criticized as one of the literature's greatest weaknesses. Since the end did not in fact come soon, these writers were wrong, and what more can be said? (see Towner 1985, 157-69). Also, when a specific number (two thousand three hundred) is provided or history is divided into periods, with the end to come in the period when one lives, a deterministic theology seems to be functioning, which would appear to make all human efforts meaningless. An element of determinism will certainly be present whenever one claims to know what the future will bring, as these writers did. Their hope was based on the firm conviction that God is sovereign and righteous, and that God's will is thus certain to prevail in the future. But some vaguely distant future would provide little hope for the suffering. "How long?" calls for the answer "Not much longer," and these writers responded that way. Theology thus has its effects on chronology.

In Daniel, the end of persecution did come soon, but it was not followed immediately by the day of resurrection (chap. 12); so he promised a bit too much. For those who cannot accept the idea that a writer of Scripture might have predicted the future incorrectly, the usual course is to claim that Daniel skips over many centuries of history between Antiochus (or the first century, if the fourth empire is identified as Rome) and the eschaton. We shall see how this expediency is used in the interpretation of chapters 9 and 11. For Daniel's readers, it was appropriate to talk about the end, for an end of some sort was in sight for them all. It might have been the end of life under torture or in battle; it might have been the end of the worship of Yahweh in Judah. Daniel insisted there would be another kind of end to the crisis, and it would be God's victory over the power of evil on earth. He did not describe the results of that victory at length, as the prophets before him had done in their eschatological texts, for he focused on an immediate crisis rather than look toward a more distant future, as they had done. For both, however, *the end* that is firmly believed to be the aim that God is working toward in human history is the end of evil (Gowan 2000, viii-xi). It has not yet come in its completeness, but believers look for and identify the signs that God is indeed at work to bring it about: among other things, in the downfall of tyrants, in the work of the Spirit to transform lives, and in the vitality of communities that struggle against the personal and social evils that still challenge the will of God.

DANIEL 9

Literary Analysis

This chapter is composed of two genres that had not appeared earlier in the book: a long prayer confessing the sins of Israel, and an account of an audition. Whereas chapters 7 and 8 continually remind the reader of what Daniel saw, this chapter refers to seeing only to identify Gabriel as the one Daniel had seen earlier. The angelic word also dominates the last section of the book, chapters 10–12.

After a brief narrative introduction (vv. 1-4*a*), the prayer (vv. 4*b*-19) introduces language and ideas that appear nowhere else in the book, which has led many commentators to conclude either that the prayer was inserted by a later redactor or that the original author made use of an already existing prayer that he did not write. Significant relationships between prayer and framework indicate that it was not a later insertion. It may be, then, that the author used a prayer known to him, but since it contains the language of Israel's worship that would have been familiar to any pious Jew, it is also possible that when a prayer of confession was called for, his own style would have been overshadowed by the language everyone used in prayer. Close parallels to this passage may be found in 1 Kgs 8:46-53; Ezra 9:6-15; Neh 9:6-37; Ps 79; Bar 1:15–3:8; Prayer of Azariah 1-22; Prayer of Manasseh. To this day there are many people whose prayer language is very traditional, using words and concepts not appearing frequently in their everyday speech and writing. To decide whether the author composed the prayer or not is not important for interpretation, but if he is responsible for including it, and it is well integrated with the rest of the chapter, as many commentators agree, then the new ideas it introduces raise significant questions.

Old Testament history is almost ignored in the rest of the book, except for references to the fall of Jerusalem and the expropriation of the Temple vessels in 1:1-2 and 5:2-3. The prayer refers to the covenant, prophets and king, the law of Moses, and the Exodus, elements of Israel's faith that typically appear in Old Testament prayers but do not appear elsewhere in Daniel. The audition will also deal with Israel's history in a cryptic way, beginning with the restoration from Exile. Elsewhere in the book the familiar Old Testament theme of Israel's sinfulness does not appear. The only Jews we hear of in chapters 1–6 are examples of faithfulness, and in chapters 7–12 Jews are the victims of evil inflicted by the archtyrant and those who cooperated with him (e.g., 11:30, 32; perhaps 9:27). The prayer, however, blames the continuing desolation of Jerusalem entirely on Israel's sinfulness. If, as suggested above, the prayer is an original part of the book, the ways it differs from the rest are not a problem of composition, but a matter to be discussed in the exegetical analysis.

The audition (vv. 24-27) is the most difficult section in the book. Of it G. R. Driver wrote:

> The reason why commentators have had recourse to these varied and often singular expedients is that, understood in the plain and obvious meaning of the words—the "week" being naturally allowed to signify a week of years—the prophecy *admits of no explanation, consistent with history, whatever*; and hence, if it is to be explained at all, an assumption, or assumptions, of some kind or other, *must* be made; and the only question that can arise is, What assumption is the least violent one, or most adequately meets the requirements of the case? (Driver 1963, 143)

Montgomery's opinion was more poetic, and equally true: "To sum up: The history of the exegesis of the 70 Weeks is the Dismal Swamp of O.T. criticism" (Montgomery 1927, 400). These verses are the result of a concern for the interpretation of Scripture which prevails in Judaism from this time on, but which appears in the Old Testament for the first time here. The chapter is introduced with Daniel's concern to understand Jeremiah's word that the devastation of Jerusalem would be fulfilled in seventy years. After Daniel's prayer, Gabriel offers a redefinition of the number seventy, then subdivides it into periods, a technique used fairly often in apocalyptic literature (note the repeated use of groups of seven in Revelation). This use of numbers would suggest precision, but they have been used by interpreters in a remarkable variety of ways. The variety is possible because the language used with the numbers is extremely vague. The exegetical analysis will describe the most important options for reading it.

Exegetical Analysis

Daniel Studies Scripture (9:1-2)

Ordinarily God communicates with Daniel by way of direct revelation, through visions and auditions, but here for once we find him pondering "the books" that contain the word of the Lord. Appeal to a written source for divine revelation is unusual in the Old Testament, except for Deuteronomy, which speaks of "this book" (28:58, 61; 29:20, 21, 27; 30:10; 31:24, 26). According to Deuteronomy the king should be a student of the book of the law (17:18-19), but Daniel is the only Old Testament character whom we find actually studying Scripture. In an earlier time, a book that claimed authority had to be authenticated by an inspired person (2 Kgs 22:8-20). By the time Daniel was written there was a functioning body of Scripture (with its exact limits as yet undefined), considered by all Jews to be the prime source of revelation, but for Daniel what was written created a problem.

Twice the book of Jeremiah speaks of seventy years. In Jer 25:11-12 the prophet says the land will become a ruin (the word used of Jerusalem in Dan 9:2) and will serve the king of Babylon for seventy years, then the king and the land of the Chaldeans will be punished. Jeremiah does not refer to the ruin or restoration of *Jerusalem* in this passage. In his letter to the exiles in Babylonia he warns them not to expect to be able to return home in the near future: "only when Babylon's seventy years are completed will I visit you, and I will fulfill to you my promise and bring you back to this place" (Jer 29:10). Jerusalem is not mentioned here, either, so it may be that Daniel's reference to its continuing desolation means that he had associated other texts (perhaps even from Isa 40–55) with the seventy-year promise of Jer 29. It is clear that Jeremiah used it as a round number. Seventy years was the full number of years that one might hope to live, according to Ps 90:10 (most people actually did well to reach forty), so the point of Jeremiah's word to the exiles was, "*You* are not going back; so make a life for yourself in Babylon." The conclusion that Jeremiah was working with a symbolic number, representing an approximate time period and never intended for exact calculation, is supported by another way that he speaks of the length of Babylonian supremacy: "All the nations shall serve him [Nebuchadnezzar] and his son and his grandson, until the time of his own land comes; then many nations and great kings shall make him their slave" (Jer 27:7).

Daniel's Prayer (9:3-19)

The number seventy leads Daniel to prayer and supplication, confessing Israel's sins and asking for mercy. The setting that the book provides for the prayer is the first year of Darius the Mede. (For the problem of identifying this Darius, see the introduction to chap. 6.) According to Dan 6:28, Darius would be replaced by Cyrus, who actually made the restoration of Jerusalem possible (Ezra 1), but Daniel shows no interest in that. Instead, chapter 9 will conclude with the unbearably depressing news—for someone living in the sixth century—that "seventy" means seventy weeks of years (70 x 7 = 490). In reality, however, the extension of seventy to four hundred ninety was intended as a message of hope, not of despair, since it was addressed to the second century, not the sixth, and the larger number was simply intended to bridge that gap.

One argument against the originality of the prayer points out that it does not ask for an explanation of Jeremiah's word (which eventually is given in vv. 24-27), but is a confession of sin. The parallels in 1 Kgs 8:46-53; Ezra 9:6-15; Neh 9:6-37 and Bar 1:15–3:8 show that this kind of prayer was a standard reaction to the fall of Jerusalem and the Exile, accepting the prophetic claim that these events were the just judgment of Israel for its sins. Daniel does not take the number seventy as a conundrum that needs to be solved, as almost all interpreters since have done. He does not "seek *answer,* as the New Revised Standard Version has it, for the verb "seek" has no object in the Hebrew text and is best understood as seeking the Lord in prayer. He reaffirms the traditional answer: Israel's sufferings continue because Israel's sinfulness continues. The dependence on tradition here is emphasized by the use of the divine name YHWH, which appears in Daniel only in this chapter (vv. 4, 8, and 14).

The language of the prayer echoes that of the Deuteronomistic literature of the Old Testament, and almost every phrase can be found elsewhere. Other commentaries contain extensive lists of the parallels, which will not be repeated here. This use of traditional language ought not to be surprising, for, as noted above, traditional language regularly appears in prayers. It is the echo of Deuteronomistic retribution theology that has raised a more important question for commentators. Unlike the rest of the book, all blame for what has gone wrong in Israel's history is ascribed to its sinfulness. A reason for that may be found in the fact that this chapter takes up a subject that is not primary in the rest of the book. It is the only chapter that focuses on the nonfulfillment of prophecy concerning Jerusalem (chaps. 8 and 11 speak only of the desecration of the sanctuary). The name "Jerusalem" occurs five times here (elsewhere only in 5:2-3, 6:10), and "the city" another five times. It is not surprising, then, especially since the prophetic word has been referred to, that the tradition concerning Jerusalem's fate as the result of divine justice appears.

More important theologically than the emphasis on sin in the prayer is the concept of God's righteousness, and that will be discussed after certain interesting details have been noted. Although Daniel is supposed to be in exile, several phrases point toward a location in Jerusalem. In verse 7 Daniel associates himself first with the people of Judah and Jerusalem, then with "those who are near and those who are far away," suggesting that he is not in exile. The first person plural in the phrase "our desolation," linked with "the city that bears your name," also suggests he lives in the city (v. 18). Although exiles are mentioned, no interest is shown in their return.

The word of the Lord was given to Israel first in the law of Moses (vv. 11 and 13) and has been transmitted through the prophets (vv. 6 and 10). Other leaders, kings, princes, and ancestors (literally "fathers") are mentioned as having failed (vv. 6 and 8), but priests are not included among them. Neither are they given credit for transmitting the Law. This may be a vague clue as to Daniel's affinities, but it is not enough to enable us to locate him specifically in second-century society. Daniel takes on the role of intercessor, as Moses and others had done before him (v. 17). The place of intercession in the Old Testament will be discussed in the theological analysis.

Two contrasting themes dominate the prayer: Israel's sin and God's righteousness. A note concerning the vocabulary of sin will suffice for the understanding of this chapter. More will need to be said about righteousness. The author uses most of the common words for sin, with one exception, which appears to be significant. Roots usually translated "sin" appear in verses 5, 8, 11, and 15; "iniquity" in verses 5 and 13; and "wickedness" in verses 5 and 15. Missing is *pešaᶜ* ("rebellion"), which might have been used in this context, as 1 Kgs 8:50 indicates. However, it does appear in verse 24, which may be a clue to the meaning of that difficult verse.

Jerusalem's sufferings are retribution for Israel's perennial sinfulness, but there is no human merit that Daniel can offer as a basis for restoration. It is sometimes said that prayers of penitence were thought to be the means by which people could reverse their fate (as in 1 Kgs 8:46-53), but Daniel claims no merit for his prayer. Although the stories depict him as apparently a perfect individual, in the prayer he associates himself with his people as deserving all the trouble that has come (v. 20). The only basis for asking God for change is to be found in God's own character, and here the key term is the root *ṣdq*, which appears in various forms in verses 7, 14, 16, and 18. Associated with it are other merciful qualities of God: steadfast love (v. 4), mercies (vv. 9 and 18), forgiveness (v. 9), and fidelity (v. 13).

It is God who is "righteous" or "right" in that his treatment of Israel has been just (vv. 7 and 14), but Israel admits there is no right on their side (v. 18), no claim they can make in the name of justice. What is "right" in the character of God is remarkable, for it is also the basis for blessing those who do not deserve it. Daniel believes that it is God's righteousness that will lead God to turn away his anger, which they deserve (v. 16). So this term that we translate "justice" and "righteousness" is also a parallel to "mercy" or "compassion" (see vv. 16 and 18). It is only for God's own sake that Daniel can hope for an answer to his prayer (vv. 17 and 19), but Israel's theology has taught him something remarkable about divine righteousness. This must be developed further in the theological analysis.

Gabriel Responds (9:20-23)

The intercessor has been confessing his own sin also, he tells us explicitly in verse 20. Then Gabriel, who had been introduced in 8:16, appears in order to explain the number seventy. Note that he is simply called a man rather than an angel (the word *mal²āk* appears only in the Aramaic part of Dan 3:28; 6:22). The supernatural figures in Daniel are not otherwise described, except for Nebuchadnezzar's statement that the fourth man in the furnace has the appearance of a son of the gods, and for an impressive depiction of the brilliance of the human figure in 10:4-6. The text of verse 21 is difficult, and scholars differ as to whether Gabriel is said to approach Daniel wearily *(y²p)* or in flight *(²ûp)*. Most think that weariness seems inappropriate for Gabriel. Angels are never described as having wings in the Old Testament, but the seraphim of Isa 6 and the cherubim of Ezek 1 do. If Gabriel is really said to be flying here, it is possible that he seemed to resemble these heavenly beings, but firm conclusions should not be drawn from a difficult text.

Daniel is to be given the gift of wisdom again (v. 22), and he will need it to understand what follows, which is called both a word and a vision (v. 23). Gabriel seems to make it clear that the prayer itself has changed nothing, for the word, which affirms God's prior decision as to when the desolation will end, already is pronounced at the beginning of Daniel's supplications.

The Seventy Weeks of Years (9:24-27)

Gabriel's response begins with a redefinition of the number seventy as meaning seventy weeks—meaning seventy times seven, that is four hundred ninety years. They will then be subdivided, with cryptic references to Israel's postexilic history, but first he ascribes meaning to that history in a series of six infinitive clauses.

to finish the transgression	to put an end to sin
to atone for iniquity	to bring in everlasting righteousness
to seal both vision and prophet	to anoint a most holy place

Verse 24 makes direct reference to the prayer in several ways. First, Gabriel's message concerns the subjects of the prayer—Daniel's people and the holy city. Next, the vocabulary chosen for the six clauses echoes the vocabulary of the prayer in significant ways. The words for sin and iniquity reappear in the second and third, righteousness appears in the fourth, and holiness in the sixth (cf. 9:16 and 17 [the New Revised Standard's "sanctuary" in v. 17 is literally "holy place"]). These references to the prayer make the choice of other words, not in the prayer, probable clues to the meaning of this difficult verse. "Transgression" *(pešaᶜ)* in the first clause appears elsewhere in Daniel only in 8:12 and 13, where it refers to the desecration of the offering. Since 9:27 refers to the same crime, the choice of this word suggests that the clause refers to Antiochus's activities. The verb *klʾ* ("finish," New Revised Standard Version) in verse 24 is not forgiveness terminology. The clause thus seems to point ahead to the "decreed end" of verse 27.

The text of the second clause is uncertain. The Masoretic Text offers two possible readings: one set of vowels would read "and to seal sins" (not impossible since the expression does occur in Job 14:17). The other set would read "and to bring sin to an end," which fits the context better, as it forms a good parallel to the previous clause. The first two clauses thus seem to belong together. The third clause could scarcely refer to Antiochus, however, since it uses the verb *kippēr* ("atone"), which is forgiveness terminology. It must be a promise of atonement of Israel's iniquity which Daniel had confessed in his prayer. This clause may then belong with the fourth, for the basis of Daniel's appeal, as noted above, was the saving righteousness of God. The "everlasting righteousness" of this clause, in keeping with the way the term is used in the prayer, would not refer to making Israel righteous, but to the manifestation of God's righteousness, which would make all the rest of the promise possible.

Clauses five and six clearly belong together as assurances that Daniel's supplications will be granted. The verb "seal" is used here with the sense of confirmation. The word "prophet" must refer to Jeremiah, whose use of the number seventy concerned Daniel. The root *qdš* had already been used of "holy city" in the introduction to this verse, and the anointing of the "holy of holies" (or "most holy place") must look beyond what is said in verse 27 to the restoration of proper worship in the Jerusalem sanctuary.

Several commentators read the six clauses as a group of three which speak of doing away with sin, and a second group of three promising restoration. The fact that "transgression" in the first clause is used elsewhere in Daniel only of Antiochus's "abomination" suggests reading the clauses in three groups of two each: the first two looking ahead to the "end" of the tyrant promised in verse 27; the next two promising the forgiveness Daniel had requested in his prayer; and the last two looking beyond what is said in verses 25-27, to the fulfillment of the decreed end (similar readings in Charles 1929, 239; and Anderson 1984, 113).

With verse 25 the subdivision of the four hundred ninety years begins, leading interpreters to the seldom resisted temptation to try to make the numbers fit an exact chronology of the postexilic period. Driver's judgment, quoted at the beginning of this section, has not been overturned, however. The "word to restore and rebuild Jerusalem" would seem at first reading to refer to Cyrus's decree (538 BC), but that produces results that satisfy no one. Some begin with Jeremiah's texts, but they are not words to restore and rebuild. A favorite date for those who are convinced the anointed one in verse 26 must be Christ is 458/7, when Artaxerxes I gave Ezra permission to lead exiles back to Jerusalem (Ezra 7:8). No rebuilding is associated with Ezra's work, but the date has been chosen because a four-hundred-ninety-year period leads to the desired end, Jesus' lifetime. The efforts to make verses 25-27 fit that period are so varied and so unsatisfactory that they will not be reviewed here.

Seventy was already a symbolic number for Jeremiah, and since numbers are regularly used for their symbolic values in apocalyptic literature, it seems best to read seventy times seven in that way here and to avoid trying to establish dates. The seven-day week and the sabbatical year were central features of Jewish practice, and the use of the number seven was extended to create the concept of the Jubilee Year, to be observed after a forty-nine-year period (Lev 25:1-7, 8-17). Daniel's four hundred ninety years represent ten of those Jubilee periods (not including the Jubilee Year itself, which is the fiftieth year). Only the beginning and end of that long period are of any interest to him—the first seven weeks (forty-nine years) and the last week. The first seven weeks are probably mentioned only because Daniel has written information about the mid–sixth century in Ezra, Haggai, and Zechariah, and that would approximately fit a seven-week period. Little is said about the intervening sixty-two weeks because they function only to fill up the symbolic number, seven times seventy. The final week is crucial, since it appears to begin with the murder of the high priest Onias III in 171 BC (see below). It locates Daniel and his readers partway through that final week, and that means the one-half week mentioned in verse 27 is also a symbolic number. Seven is the perfect number; half of seven would mean only a short time remains before the end.

The language of verses 25-27 is extremely vague compared with the rest of the book, but if it is agreed that the subject-matter is the same as that of chapters 7, 8, and 11, most of what is said is a good fit with what is known about the activities of Antiochus IV Epiphanes. The only detail mentioned to mark off the end of the first seven weeks is the appearance of an anointed prince. This best fits the high priest Joshua (or Jeshua; Ezra 3; Hag 1:12; 2:2; Zech 3), since the high priest was anointed in the postexilic period and the term *nâgîd* "prince" is used of Temple officials in Chronicles and Nehemiah. It seems a bit strange that the Temple is not mentioned in connection with the rebuilding of Jerusalem in verse 25 but it is present in verse 26.

The presence of the word *māšîaḥ* ("anointed one") in verses 25 and 26 has led many Christians to insist this must refer to Jesus, and to adjust the chronology so as to lead to the first century AD. Both occurrences of the word *māšîaḥ* most naturally fit high priests. In the midst of the negotiations between the hellenizing party in Jerusalem and Antiochus IV Epiphanes, the high priest Onias III, who resisted those negotiations, was murdered (171 BC; 2 Macc 4:34-38). The last week of years begins with his death (v. 26). The rest of verse 26 speaks of the effects of the turmoil on Jerusalem early in this period. The city was not destroyed, as the verb *yašḥît* has been translated, but the word can sometimes mean "damage" (1 Sam 8:5; 2 Kgs 18:25), and that is appropriate here (1 Macc 1:20-35; 2 Macc 5:11-21). The covenant in verse 27 is, then, the agreement between Antiochus and the "reforming party," which gave Jerusalem a charter as a hellenistic city and led to the introduction of Greek institutions (e.g., the *ephebeion* [guild of young men]), *boule* [council of elders], and gymnasium [1 Macc 1:11-15; 1 Macc 4:9-15]). As a result of continuing unrest in Jerusalem, Antiochus proscribed the practice of Judaism and introduced the pollution of the Temple, described here and in 11:31 as the "abomination that makes desolate," and as the "transgression *(pešaᶜ)* that makes desolate" in 8:13 (1 Macc 1:54-59; 2 Macc 6:1-2). As in 8:25, the resolution of the crisis is announced with the greatest brevity: "until the decreed end is poured out upon the desolator." For suffering people, the only important question is "Will there be an end?" The numbers (two thousand three hundred in 8:14 and one-half week of years here in this chapter) together with the insistence on divine determination of history (vv. 23, 24, and 27), are intended to offer a certain answer.

Theological and Ethical Analysis

This chapter introduces a tradition of great importance for the history of Judaism and Christianity: the appeal to Scripture as a source for understanding what God is doing in the world. Daniel has access to "the books," a collection of written works that he considers to be authoritative, since he found in them "the word of the Lord" to Jeremiah. Acceptance of books as a source of authoritative, divine revelation may be found in Neh 8–9, where, as a part of the public reading of Scripture, interpretation of some sort was added, "so that the people understood the reading" (Neh 8:7-8). Not everything in these books was easy to understand, and some of it was troublesome, so various methods of interpretation had already been developed by the time Dan 9 was written. The book of Jubilees, for example, retells Gen 1–Exod 14 making sure that it says what it ought to say. The "commentaries" found at Qumran were written with the assumption that Scripture predicted the events of their own time, so that what was called for was identification of whom the text really referred to. The oral law of the Pharisees was developed in part through the use of interpretive techniques for extending the ethical teachings of the Torah to new situations.

In Dan 9, interpretation involves the redefinition of what a number means: not seventy years but seventy weeks of years. This is not exegesis, for there is nothing in the text of Jeremiah to justify it. It involves a new claim of authority, "a word" (v. 23), presumably from God, and transmitted by Gabriel. Note that every interpretive process brings to Scripture some outside claim of authority, so that *sola Scriptura* is slightly misleading. The authors of Jubilees and the Qumran commentaries knew what the Bible should say and their interpretations made sure it did say that. The same thing must be said about some contemporary "liberal" as well as fundamentalist readings. For those who wish to be truly open to serious consideration of *whatever* Scripture may say, however, it is important always to be self-critical, aware of what one's chosen methods, presuppositions, and desires may be introducing, whether or not they are justified by the text. Daniel claimed divine intervention for his free, new interpretation. The contemporary reader may not do that explicitly, but needs to be always modest about claims to truth, lest it happen implicitly.

There is a very interesting tradition of intercessory prayer in the Old Testament, of which Dan 9 is a part. The most important parallels to his prayer are to be found in the prayers of Moses, since both appealed for mercy on a people who had nothing to commend them. In Exod 32, immediately after the sealing of the covenant at Sinai, the people make and worship a golden calf. God proposes to destroy the lot of them and start over with Moses, but Moses attempts—successfully—to change God's mind (32:7-14). He can appeal to nothing in the people worth saving; the three motives he offers all have to do with God himself (see also Num 14:13-19). The question of whether a disobedient people can have any future as the people of God occupies God and Moses for some time, with the basis for the future finally appearing in God's own self-definition:

> The LORD, the LORD,
> a God merciful and gracious,
> slow to anger,
> and abounding in steadfast love and faithfulness,
> keeping steadfast love for the thousandth generation,

forgiving iniquity and transgression and sin,
yet by no means clearing the guilty,
but visiting the iniquity of the parents
upon the children
and the children's children,
to the third and the fourth generation. (Exod 34:6-7)

Abraham's intercession on behalf of Sodom, in Gen 18:23-33, is not as close a parallel to Dan 9, for he assumes that if there are righteous people in the city, God will save the wicked for the sake of the righteous. That is a striking idea, but it does not go as far as the prayers of Moses and Daniel, since for them the only righteousness is to be found in God. They do not, for example claim righteousness for themselves as intercessors, nor do they assume a privileged status. Both acknowledge themselves willing to be judged with the guilty (Exod 32:31-32; Dan 9:20). What is most remarkable about these prayers, then, is their insistence that *justice*, as practiced by the God of Israel, transcends human understanding. Somehow it includes forgiving the guilty, redeeming those who do not deserve to be redeemed. There is no indication in Exod 32–34 of any act of repentance on the part of the people—it is all between Moses and God!

Daniel asks God to restore "for God's own sake" (9:17, 19). This echoes the sole basis Ezekiel could affirm for his promises of redemption. At one point in the book, Ezekiel appeals to his people to change their ways, assuring them that if they do, forgiveness is possible (chap. 18). However, in his view of the future, nothing depends on human merit. It is all because God wills it that there will be a new Israel (36:22-33), and repentance will be the result of, not the reason for, salvation (16:60-61; 39:25-29). This is also the basis for Daniel's hope.

Daniel uses the key word ṣĕdāqâ in a remarkable way that is paralleled by a few other Old Testament texts. Usually, prayer language uses the word in its forensic sense, corresponding to our understanding of justice. God is asked to judge the wicked for their sins and to deliver the righteous (e.g., Pss 17:1-5; 119:153-60). But the root ṣdq and related roots, špṭ, dyn, and ryb, all of which have to do with judging, were also used emphatically to affirm God's care for the physically helpless (e.g., Pss 9:8-9; 10:17-18; 103:6) and to place that care upon the conscience of Israel as well (Ps 82:3; Prov 31:8-9; Jer 22:3). In a few passages this divine concern for the weak is extended to include the spiritually helpless (i.e., the guilty):

> I have not hidden your saving help [ṣidqātĕkā] within my heart, . . .
> Do not, O LORD, withhold
>   your mercy from me;
> let your steadfast love and your faithfulness
>   keep me safe forever.
> For evils have encompassed me
>   without number;
> my iniquities have overtaken me,
>   until I cannot see.
>
> (Ps 40:10*a*, 11-12*a*)

The psalmist asks for divine help because of his sins, not because of his righteousness, and associates God's righteousness with mercy, steadfast love, and faithfulness.

Psalm 143 is more explicit in confessing the psalmist's unworthiness and total dependence on God's mercy:

> Hear my prayer, O LORD;
>   give ear to my supplications in your faithfulness;
>   answer me in your righteousness [ṣidqātekā].
> Do not enter into judgment with your servant,
>   for no one living is righteous before you.
> For your name's sake, O LORD, preserve my life.
> In your righteousness bring me out of trouble. (Ps 143:1-2, 11)

The most remarkable of these texts is Micah 7:9, since it uses three of the four roots mentioned above in the sense of deliverance rather than judgment:

> I must bear the indignation of the LORD,
>   because I have sinned against him,
> until he takes my side [yārîb rîbî]
>   and executes judgment for me [ʿāśâ mišpāṭ].
> He will bring me out to the light;
>   I shall see his vindication [ṣidqātô].

These are prayers of individuals who confess that, because of their sinfulness, they have nothing to offer but a plea for help, apparently reasoning that God's concern for the weak extends also to the spiritually weak. The same reasoning appears in Dan 9. He admits that "because of our sins and the iniquities of our ancestors, Jerusalem and your people have become a disgrace among all our neighbors" (v. 16). He asks God to turn away his anger according to his *ṣidqôt*, acknowledging they have no *ṣidqôt* on which to base this plea, but depending solely on God's great mercy (v. 18).

> *Ṣdqh* is not a justice that is concerned above all to see wrongdoing punished. It is a concern for what is right that rejoices in being merciful to the weak; and those who suffer as a consequence of sin are still seen as those who suffer and need to be restored. (Goldingay 1989, 243)

A few Old Testament texts thus already contain intimations of the concept of God's righteousness, which acquits the guilty for God's own sake, better known from Paul's writings:

> But now, apart from law, the righteousness of God has been disclosed, and is attested by the law and the prophets, the righteousness of God through faith in Jesus Christ for all who believe. For there is no distinction, since all have sinned and fall short of the glory of God; they are now justified by his grace as a gift, through the redemption that is in Christ Jesus, whom God put forward as a sacrifice of atonement by his blood, effective through faith. He did this to show his righteousness, because in his divine forbearance he had passed over the sins previously committed; it was to prove at the present time that he himself is righteous and that he justifies the one who has faith in Jesus. (Rom 3:21-26)

DANIEL 10–12

Literary Analysis

The last three chapters of Daniel comprise a single unit, with a framework composed of visionary elements enclosing a lengthy audition. Chapter 10 through 11:1 is entirely introductory, and one of the questions for exegesis is the need to account for such an elaborate introduction to the message itself. The conclusion (12:5-13) raises the "How long?" question again (cf. 7:25; 8:13-14), and might be considered an appendix to the book except for the reappearance of conversation involving Daniel and supernatural figures, as in chapter 10.

The chapter divisions are thus somewhat unfortunate, in that they tend to disguise the structure of this long unit. A more appropriate division into chapters would have included 10:1–11:1 as the introduction, 11:2–12:4 as the body, and 12:5-13 as the conclusion.

The introduction and conclusion are relatively simple accounts of visions. They are not symbolic like those in chapters 7 and 8, for what is seen—supernatural figures—is not interpreted. For the most part we are told only that Daniel sees "men." The truly visual element appears only in 10:4-6. The magnificent figure with a gleaming body and a rumbling voice is described in terms strongly reminiscent of the way Ezekiel described his vision of the throne chariot of the Lord (Ezek 1). A great deal is made of the profound way the appearance affects Daniel physically (10:8-11, 15-17), as he faints and requires supernatural help to get to his hands and knees, and finally to stand. He even loses his ability to speak. These features are familiar parts of the vision genre (cf. 8:18, 27; 7:15, 28), with precedents in Isa 6 and Ezek 1:28–2:2; 3:15, 25-26, and they seem to be accurate reflections of the actual experiences of visionaries. Some parallels to the call-genre have been noted (cf. Exod 3–4, which exemplifies the genre as containing an encounter with the divine, a commission, a reaction, and a divine rejoinder), but they are imperfect and do not seem to be significant in this context.

The body of the passage takes up history again, but in a new way. Unlike the brief and often vague survey provided in 9:24-27, a great deal of accurate detail is provided concerning the relationship between the Ptolemaic and Seleucid dynasties, and the effects those governments had on the Jewish people. The symbolism of chapters 2, 7, and 8 is missing, but the mysterious tone that characterizes all apocalyptic literature is provided here by the use of "king of the south" and "king of the north" rather than the names of the rulers in question. The names can all be provided from other sources. This purports to be a prediction of future events, but is best understood as history writing, as far as 11:39. With verse 40 actual prediction begins. This is a unique way of writing history, for the Old Testament. The publication of the Dynastic Prophecy and related texts provides evidence that Daniel may have used a genre familiar to him from Babylonian literature (Grayson 1975, 3-37; Delcor 1993, 365-86). The Dynastic Prophecy is very fragmentary but appears to be a supposed prediction of the rise and fall of empires—Assyrian, Babylonian, Persian (called Elam), and Greek (called Hanaean). As in Dan 11, the air of mystery is created by the refusal to name any of the kings.

The real interest of this long account is the same as in chapters 7–9, the fate of the archtyrant, and the fate is announced with brevity: "Yet he shall come to his end, with no one to help him" (11:45). Something unparalleled is added in 12:1-4, however. Eschatology proper had appeared in the briefest way, in the promise of an eternal kingdom in 2:44 and 7:27. A new eschatological promise is offered in 12:2-3. The idea of the kingdom does not reappear, but resurrection of the dead and the glorification of "the wise" is promised. These subjects will be elaborated greatly in other apocalyptic works, often in visionary form, but here they are simply announced briefly as the conclusion of the "future-history" genre.

Exegetical Analysis

The Appearance of a Heavenly Being (10:1-9)

Earlier, Daniel's tenure was said to last until the first year of Cyrus (1:21). If that is understood to mean it continued into the reign of Cyrus rather than ending with his first year, then the reference to his third year in 10:1 need not be taken as a discrepancy. Although there are some visionary elements in this section, note that this is emphatically a verbal communication, with "word" used three times in one verse. The "word" is modified by verbs meaning to reveal and to understand, and is called true

(v. 2). A fourth modifier, ṣābāʾ, is more difficult. It has been translated host (since it is used of the heavenly hosts elsewhere),
appointed time, conflict, and task or service. It may refer to the
heavenly and earthly conflict of which the succeeding verses speak.

Daniel says he had been mourning for three weeks during the
first month of the year. This would be Nisan (March-April), the
month of the feasts of Unleavened Bread and Passover. Normally,
fasting during those times would be improper, but perhaps this
reflects the actual experience of the second-century visionary during the persecution, when observance of Passover would have been
forbidden. As in chapter 8, his vision occurs by the bank of a river.
Since much in chapter 10 is closely related to the visions of Ezekiel,
the choice of setting may have been influenced by the fact that his
inaugural vision took place by the river Chebar (Ezek 1:1).

Daniel sees "a man" whose appearance is so awe-inspiring that
he faints. The man is never named, but many commentators think
he is Gabriel, who spoke to Daniel in chapter 8. There are several reasons for doubting that, the foremost of which is that if
Daniel knew it was the Gabriel he had seen earlier, surely he
would have named him here. Also, if Gabriel looked like this, one
would expect the description to be in chapter 8 when he first
appeared to Daniel. His appearance did lead Daniel to faint in
chapter 8, but the figure in chapter 10 has an even more profound
effect on him. So we shall leave the figure unnamed. He is dressed
in linen, like the man Ezekiel saw in his vision of Jerusalem (Ezek
9:3; 10:6), but the effect on the eye is that of astounding brilliance.
This is the traditional way of attempting to describe the presence
of heavenly beings: using words for bright light, fire, polished metals, and precious stones. The terms used in verse 6, including
"roar of a multitude," all occur in Ezekiel's vision of the throne
chariot (Ezek 1:7, 13, 16, 24). Both Ezekiel and Daniel fainted
and were struck dumb by the sight (Ezek 1:28; 3:15, 26; Dan
10:8-9, 15).

Daniel Is Prepared for the Revelation (10:10–11:1)

Strength and reassurance are provided by a mysterious hand
and voice, both presumably belonging to the figure just described

(vv. 10-12). God's concern for Daniel is conveyed not only by calling him "greatly beloved," but also by assuring him that this messenger had been commissioned at the very beginning of Daniel's fast. The same assurance had been offered with reference to his prayer in 9:23, but in this case twenty-one days have elapsed, so an explanation for the delay is offered. The explanation introduces ideas concerning the supernatural world which are mostly new to the Old Testament. (See the theological and ethical analysis.)

It will be useful to describe the cast of characters at this point. The principle speaker from 10:10 through 12:4 is presumably the unnamed figure who was described in 10:5-6. He refers to three persons called princes: the prince of Persia (10:13, 20); Michael, "one of the chief princes" (10:13), also called "your prince" (10:21); and the prince of Greece (10:20). In this book they remain offstage and seem to be mentioned only to account for the delay in responding to Daniel's fast. These passing references to battles in the spiritual realm must be evidence that such ideas were already well known when the book was written. The one in human form who touches Daniel again and continues to speak to him (10:18-19) must be the man clothed in linen who appeared in verse 5; so at this point Daniel has seen one figure and heard about three others. Two new figures appear in 12:5, with a question for the man clothed in linen. Since the interpreter in chapters 8 and 9 was Gabriel, the temptation to identify this very prominent speaker as Gabriel is understandable; but note that the interpreter in chapter 7 is also anonymous.

This lengthy introduction does not seem to contribute much to the message of the passage as a whole. Nothing is made of the battle among the princes in the message that follows in chapter 11. The description of the heavenly figure and of Daniel's reaction to his appearance is probably intended to emphasize the divine origin of the message to follow. Its contents are of the same kind as the messages he had received earlier: "What is to happen to your people at the end of days" (10:14). The reliability of the prediction is emphasized at the end of the introduction: "But I am to tell you what is inscribed in the book of truth" (10:21). Several books are mentioned in Daniel, and this one appears to function differently from those in 7:10 and 12:1. Here Daniel learns everything that is to happen has already been written down in heaven.

Conflict Between the Ptolemies and Seleucids (11:2-20)

The succession of empires in chapters 2 and 7 began with Babylonia but it no longer appears in chapters 8 and 11, which begin with Persia and move quickly to the hellenistic kingdoms that followed Alexander the Great. Only four kings are assigned to Persia, so most of the history of the sixth to fourth centuries has been condensed. Four Persian kings are mentioned in the Bible—Cyrus, Darius, Xerxes, and Artaxerxes—and that may be the reason for the number in verse 2, which seems to be just a vague summary of the period. The exploits of Alexander are of no great interest, either (vv. 3-4), and he is passed over quickly in order to recount the fortunes of the kings who ruled or tried to rule Palestine.

The details of the ensuing history are without theological interest, and the biblical text can probably be made most readable by placing it in a column parallel to an account that includes names and dates.

verse 5 Then the king of the south shall grow strong, but one of his officers shall grow stronger than he and shall rule a realm greater than his own realm.

Ptolemy I occupied Egypt and Phoenicia/Palestine. Seleucus I conquered Babylonia and Syria. Their allies agreed he should have Phoenicia/Palestine, leading to sporadic attempts by the Seleucids to occupy it.

verse 6 After some years they shall make an alliance, and the daughter of the king of the south shall come to the king of the north to ratify the agreement. But she shall not retain her power, and his offspring shall not endure.

After unsuccessful campaigns by Ptolemy II and Antiochus II, a peace treaty was sealed by a diplomatic marriage of Ptolemy's daughter, Berenice, to Antiochus II (252 or 250 BC). He divorced his first wife, Laodice, and barred her sons Seleucus and Antiochus from succession to the throne. But

She shall be given up, she and her attendants and her child and the one who supported her. In those times

Laodice murdered Berenice and her infant son, and shortly after that Antiochus II died, probably poisoned by her. Her son became king Seleucus II (246 BC).

verses 7-8 a branch from he roots shall rise up in his place. He shall come against the army and enter the fortress of the king of the north, and he shall take action against them and prevail. Even their gods, with their precious vessels of silver and gold, he shall carry off to Egypt as spoils of war. For some years he shall refrain from attacking the king of the north;

Ptolemy III, Berenice's brother, came to the throne and, in revenge for her death, campaigned successfully against Seleucus II, ranging far into Asia, but was called back to Egypt, and Seleucus regained his territory.

verse 9 then the latter shall invade the realm of the king of the south, but will return to his own land.

In 242 Seleucus II attempted to invade Palestine and was repulsed.

verse 10 His sons shall wage war and assemble a multitude of great forces, which shall advance like a flood and pass through, and again shall carry the war as far as his fortress.

The sons were Seleucus III (225–223) and Antiochus III the Great (223–187).

verses 11-12 Moved with rage, the king of the south shall go out and do battle against the king of the north, who shall muster

Antiochus III invaded Palestine in 217 and got as far as Raphia (on the southern border), where he was defeated by Ptolemy IV.

a great multitude, which shall, however, be defeated by his enemy. When the multitude has been carried off, his heart shall be exalted, and he shall overthrow tens of thousands, but he shall not prevail.

verses 13 For the king of the north shall again raise a multitude, larger than the former, and after some years he shall advance with a great army and abundant supplies.

Between 212 and 205 Antiochus III was occupied with subduing the eastern parts of his empire.

verses 14 In those times many shall rise against the king of the south. The lawless among your own people shall lift themselves up in order to fulfill the vision, but they shall fail.

Ptolemy IV was succeeded by Ptolemy V, who was only four years old, with resulting factions at court. "The lawless" may be the pro-Seleucid party among the Jews in Jerusalem, since Daniel is clearly anti-Seleucid.

verses 15-17 Then the king of the north shall come and throw up siegeworks, and take a well-fortified city. And the forces of the south shall not stand, not even his picked troops, for there shall be no strength to resist. But he who comes against him shall take the actions he pleases, and no one shall withstand him. He shall take a position in the beautiful land, and all of it shall be in his power.

Antiochus III invaded Phoenicia/Palestine successfully, defeating the Egyptian army at Paneas, and besieging Sidon until it fell.

Palestine came finally under Seleucid control in 199.

He shall set his mind to come with the strength of his whole kingdom, and he shall bring terms of peace and perform them. In order to destroy the kingdom, he shall give him a woman in marriage; but it shall not succeed or be to his advantage.

Antiochus gave his daughter Cleopatra in marriage to Ptolemy V, but it was not "to his advantage," since she loyally supported her husband.

verse 18 Afterward he shall turn to the coastlands, and shall capture many. But a commander shall put an end to his insolence; indeed, he shall turn his insolence back upon him.

Antiochus III then turned toward the northwest, campaigning in Asia Minor and reaching as far as Thermopylae in 191, where he was defeated by the Romans. They drove him out of Asia Minor after his defeat at Magnesia in 190.

verse 19 Then he shall turn back toward the fortresses of his own land, but he shall stumble and fall, and shall not be found.

Antiochus III died in the east while attempting to sack the temple at Elymas to get resources to pay tribute to Rome.

verse 20 Then shall arise in his place one who shall send an official for the glory of the kingdom; but within a few days he shall be broken, though not in anger or in battle.

Antiochus III was succeeded by Seleucus IV (187–175), whose tribute-collector Heliodorus (2 Macc 3) is probably the official referred to. Seleucus was murdered by Heliodorus, and his brother Antiochus IV took the throne since his son Demetrius, the true heir, was a hostage in Rome.

The Career of Antiochus IV Epiphanes (11:21-45)

The archtyrant is introduced with an insult ("contemptible person") and a reference to the irregularity of his accession to
the throne. The complex history of affairs in Jerusalem that eventually led to the decree proscribing the practice of Judaism is
alluded to very briefly in verses 22-23. (For details, see Bickerman
1962, 93-111; Tcherikover 1961, 152-203; Schürer 1973, 137-63.)
In brief, a "reforming party" made up of some of the influential
men in Jerusalem sought to gain for that city the commercial
advantages that other cities in the Near East enjoyed as a result of
new charters converting their governments to the form of the
hellenistic *polis*. The prince of the covenant who was swept away
(v. 22) was the high priest Onias III, who opposed these efforts.
The hellenizers offered the emperor a suitable bribe, Onias was
deposed, and Jason was appointed to be the new high priest
(1 Macc 1:11-15; 2 Macc 4:7-20). This is the alliance with a small
party referred to in verse 25. Onias was later murdered (2 Macc
4:34). Verse 24 speaks in general terms of Antiochus's early military successes, then his first campaign against Egypt is described
in verses 25-27. He defeated his nephew Ptolemy VI (son of
Cleopatra), and after an apparently friendly meeting with him at
Memphis (v. 27) subjugated Egypt to himself and plundered it.
First Maccabees 1:20-28 suggests he plundered Jerusalem on his
return from this first campaign, which might correspond to "his
heart shall be set against the holy covenant" (v. 28), but this is not
supported by 2 Macc 4:21-23, which speaks of a peaceful visit.

His second invasion of Egypt (168) was a disastrous turning
point for the Jews (vv. 29-30). These campaigns were in violation
of the treaty imposed on his father, Antiochus III, by the Romans
at Magnesia, so Ptolemy VI appealed to them for help. Daniel
calls the Romans "Kittim," a term regularly used of them in
Hebrew at this period. They sent Gaius Popillius Laenas, who met
Antiochus as he neared the Egyptian capital, handed him a tablet
containing a Roman senate resolution requiring Antiochus to
evacuate Egypt, then with his staff drew a circle in the sand
around the king, demanding a yes or no answer before the king
could step out of the circle. Antiochus succumbed; his designs on

Egypt were ended. On his humiliating return home, he found insurrection in Jerusalem. Jason had been replaced as high priest by Menelaus, but upon hearing a rumor that Antiochus was dead Jason attacked the city (2 Macc 5:1-8). Antiochus's troops took the city by storm, gave control back to Menelaus, and plundered the Temple treasury (2 Macc 5:11-21; Dan 11:30b-31a; perhaps 1 Macc 1:20-28). He left troops quartered in the city, which resulted in continued unrest. This seems to explain the decree abolishing the Jewish religion. He recognized that the unrest centered around the Temple and priesthood, so decided to replace it with his own cult. Detailed parallels to verses 31-35 appear in 1 Macc 1:41-64 and 2 Macc 5:22-6:11. The "wise" whom Daniel refers to must be the group of faithful Jews to which he belongs (vv. 33 and 35), some of whom had been martyred when he wrote this book. At this point 1 and 2 Maccabees introduce the family of Mattathias, who will become the heroes of those books because of the successful rebellion led by Judas Maccabeus (1 Macc 2; 2 Macc 5:27). If Daniel mentions the Maccabees at all, it is in verse 34, with "they shall receive a little help," so he does not seem to favor the violent resistance that began at that time.

The passage that follows (vv. 36-39) is not the chronological successor to the preceding verses but is a general condemnation of Antiochus. A good deal was written about him by the classical authors, for they found him to be both fascinating and shocking, both generous and cruel, insisting on glorifying himself but enjoying at times the company of commoners (Polybius, *History* xxvi 1; xxx 25-27). He did "exalt himself," claiming to be an epiphany of Zeus on earth. We need not try to make all the details of these verses fit what is known of his behavior from other sources, for the details represent a theological judgment of him made by Daniel.

With verse 40 the author ventures upon prediction of what is the real future for him. This makes it possible to date the final form of the book perhaps more accurately than any other book of the Bible. History has been described with great accuracy as far as Antiochus's second campaign against Egypt and his subsequent actions against the Jews in Palestine. In verse 40, however, a third campaign against Egypt, leading to his death on the Mediterranean coast, is described, and nothing like this happened. There was no attack by the king of the south, and instead of moving against Egypt, in 166 or 165 Antiochus campaigned in Armenia and Persia. In March of 164 he issued an edict of toleration, bringing persecution of the Jews to an end. Sacrifice in the Temple was restored in December of 164, and Antiochus died in Persia sometime that winter (1 Macc 6:1-17; 2 Macc 9:1-26). The author knows nothing of those events, so 11:40-45 must be real prediction, and his work can be dated between what was for him actual past and present (11:2-39) and what was actual future (11:40–12:3). Chapter 11 and probably the final form of the entire book can thus be dated between 166 and early 164. The author is partly right in his prediction, however, in saying the tyrant's end is near, and that was the most important part of it. He does not know that persecution actually would end before Antiochus's death, with the edict of toleration in March of 164.

At verse 40 (and sometimes as early as v. 21) some interpreters have claimed Daniel is no longer speaking of the Seleucids but has skipped over many centuries, from the second century BC to the last days, and has introduced the antichrist (e.g., Jerome; see Archer 1977, 129; Young 1949, 251; Miller 1994, 305-13). So Daniel the prophet was not mistaken, after all. This defense of Daniel's accuracy raises several unanswered questions. Why would a sixth-century prophet recount in great detail the fates of a series of third- and second-century kings—meaningless history—then without warning or explanation skip to the antichrist? Antichrist is at any rate a concept that first appeared in the New Testament (1 John 2:18, 22; 4:3; 2 John 7). It was greatly elaborated in later Christian writings, but it is a completely unhistorical approach to project it back into the Old Testament.

Vindication (12:1-4)

Something completely new is added to Daniel's last message concerning the future. Two of his messages said nothing about the destiny of the righteous, concluding only with the assurance that the end of the archtyrant's rule was certain (8:25; 9:27). Two spoke of an eternal kingdom that was to come (2:44; 7:27), and the latter spoke of the "people of the holy ones of the Most High." The main promise of the visions was that suffering was near its end, and the author scarcely looked beyond the fulfillment of that hope. It may be significant that the idea of eternal kingdom appears only in the pre-Seleucid material of chapter 2 and in the vision of chapter 7, which appears to be dated before the desecration of the Temple. The intensity of the persecution after that may have made such a hope less meaningful.

The deaths of the martyrs raised serious questions concerning the sovereignty and justice of God. The insistence of every chapter from 7 through 11 on the certainty that the rule of the tyrant would end soon was an answer to the sovereignty question, but the justice question remained in the air when too many of the righteous died before the tyrant. So the claim is now made for God's sovereignty even over death, that justice may be made manifest.

We cannot project Daniel's promise of resurrection into the distant future, as we would like, since he connects it specifically with the last days of Antiochus IV Epiphanes: "At that time . . . ." The climax will come with Michael taking his stand, presumably in order to prevail over the "prince" who represents the Seleucids in the spiritual realm, noting what is said of him in 10:13, 21. The time of terrible anguish probably does not refer to new sufferings after Antiochus's death, for that would contradict the sense of the other visions. It probably refers to the continuing anguish described in chapter 11, now explicitly promising deliverance for the righteous, "everyone who is found written in the book." Daniel appears to refer to several different concepts of heavenly records. In 7:10 the books seem to contain the indictments of the world empires. In 10:21 the book of truth contains the account of what will happen in history. This book appears to be the one called the "book of life" elsewhere; the list of the names of those who belong to the covenant community (Exod 32:32-33; Ps 69:28; Mal 3:16-18). The point in speaking of such a heavenly record is to offer assurance that every righteous person is known to God and will not be forgotten.

Death and resurrection are spoken of in terms of "sleep" and "awakening," as in a few other places (Job 14:12; Jer 51:39, 57; both denying resurrection). The closest parallel to Dan 12:2 is Isa 26:19: "Your dead shall live, their corpses shall rise. O dwellers in the dust, awake and sing for joy!" There is debate about whether this verse speaks of the resurrection of the individual or whether it uses resurrection as a metaphor for the restoration of Israel, as in Ezek 37:1-14. Daniel, however, clearly speaks of the resurrection of individuals. The term "many" has been much discussed, since many interpreters would like to find general resurrection here, but the grammar of the verse does not permit converting "many" to "all." It is the justice question that governs Daniel's language. For those who have been treated justly in this life, the old Israelite view of life and death is apparently still adequate. However, even after death, something must—and will—be done about those who have suffered unjustly or sinned without punishment.

An argument has been made, based on the double use of "these" in verse 2 (in Hebrew; "some" in the NRSV), that only the first "these" refers to the ones who will be raised—to eternal life. The second "these" would then speak of the ones not raised, left in shame and eternal contempt (Alfrink 1959, 355-71; Hartman and Di Lella 1978, 308; Lacocque 1979, 243-44). Some support for this may be found in the use of *dirʾôn* ("contempt") for the wicked, since it occurs elsewhere only in Isa 66:24, with reference to dead bodies. Most scholars believe the text speaks of a double resurrection, however. The eternal kingdom of chapters 2 and 7 has been replaced by eternal life for individuals. In neither case does the word *ʿôlām* mean "eternity" in our sense of timeless. The Hebrew concept is that of a very long time, but perhaps without a measurable end.

A key word for Daniel to identify the righteous, the group to which he evidently belongs, is *maśkîl*, one of the words meaning wise. He has spoken of their work to teach "the many" and of their sufferings, "so that they may be refined, purified and cleansed," in 11:33-35. The word is used of those who will be blessed in the future in 12:3, 10. It seems likely that he thought of them as fulfilling the work of the Suffering Servant in Isa 52:13–53:12 (Ginsberg 1953, 400-4). The beginning of the song is usually translated, "See, my servant shall prosper," but "prosper" is another of the meanings of *śkl*, the root of *maśkîl*, so this may account for Daniel's choice of that noun to designate the faithful group. He says they "lead many to righteousness," and a similar expression is used of the Servant in Isa 53:11. In somewhat cryptic terms, the prophet speaks of vindication and life after death for the Servant (53:8-12), and this may well have provided the scriptural basis for Daniel's hope for resurrection for the *maśkîlim*. Although Daniel's timing was wrong, Judaism accepted the hope for vindication after death, and it was developed at length as early as c. 100 BC, in Wis 2:12–3:9 (note an echo of Dan 12:3 in Wis 3:7).

Since the visions of Daniel were newly produced in the second century but claimed to come from a sixth-century character, the idea that the book had been kept hidden for all those years is proposed to account for the fact that no one had known any of this previously (12:4). This reminds the author of a saying from Amos concerning a time when the word of the Lord will be unavailable (Amos 8:11-12), and Daniel alludes to that: "Many shall be running back and forth, and evil (so the Septuagint; the Masoretic Text has "knowledge") shall increase."

The Postscript: How Much Longer? (12:5-13)

Daniel is still by the river Tigris, where we found him in 10:4. Now he overhears a conversation between two unnamed figures and joins in eventually. This passage parallels 8:13-14 in several respects. Both are set beside a river and involve two anonymous figures asking and answering the question "How long?" The answer given in 8:13—2,300 evenings and mornings—does not reappear, but instead three other answers are given. The first comes from the vision in chapter 7: "time, two times, and half a time" (12:7; 7:25). A specific beginning point is given in verse 11—"from the time that the regular burnt offering is taken away and the abomination that desolates is set up" (December 6, 167; cf. 8:13; 1 Macc 1:54)—but now a different time period is indicated (1,290 days) and another is immediately added in verse 12 (1,335 days). For careful discussion of these numbers, based on what is known of the calendars in use at the time, G. R. Driver's article may be consulted (Driver 1963, 62-90). The chief value of the article is the evidence it provides, that there is no clearly correct explanation for the various numbers. The persecution itself lasted less than three and one-half years (until December 14, 164; 1 Macc 4:52) and less than the 1,150 days of 8:13, so the numbers in 12:11-12 may be referring to the expected resurrection, which had not yet occurred when the epilogue was written. However, there is no indication that the prediction of Antiochus's death had yet been fulfilled. Proposals that the numbers are based on the use of different calendars, or that they represent successive updatings because an earlier date had passed, explain very little.

Finally, Daniel is offered a blessing. "Rest," in this context probably means death, since rising for his reward at the end of days clearly is a promise that he will share in the resurrection of the wise promised in 12:8. The book began with wisdom stories, with young men chosen for privilege because of their wisdom (chap. 1), and with accounts of Daniel's successes because of this divine gift. Wisdom has come to mean something more in the latter chapters. It may lead to suffering and death rather than prosperity. It is a gift that those who possess it are to convey to "the many"; so the wise have become servants with a mission (11:33; 12:3). Rewards for the wise may come at great cost, but they are certain, for wisdom itself, the strength to persevere, and victory even over death are the gifts of the God of Israel.

Theological and Ethical Analysis

Daniel represents an early stage in the development of angelology. The Hebrew word *mal'āk*, meaning "messenger," was translated by *angelos* in Greek, from which our word "angel" is derived. Some of the messengers in the Old Testament are clearly human (e.g., Isa 14:32; 18:2; 30:4), but others equally clearly are supernatural beings. For example, in Gen 22:11, the *mal'āk* of the Lord spoke from heaven and ascended in the flame of Manoah's altar in Judg 13:20. Seldom is any description of these beings provided, except to say that they are human in appearance. Daniel refers to them as "men"; the Prince of the army of the Lord in Josh 5:13-14 is also called a man. Ezekiel saw "men" in his visions (Ezek 9:1-2; 40:3). Later descriptions of angels with wings may have developed from assimilating them to other heavenly beings in the Old Testament, since both the seraphim of Isa 6 and the cherubim of Ezek 1 had wings (cf. the cherubim on the ark of the covenant, Exod 25:20). The *mal'ākîm* appear fairly often in Old Testament narrative, but seldom in the prophetic books. The only significant uses of the word to refer to supernatural creatures are in Zech 1–6 and Mal 2:7; 3:1. Even Daniel uses it only in 3:28 and 6:23, and never of the beings in chapters 7–12. Interpreters always call them angels, however, since Gabriel and Michael are so designated in the New Testament and other contemporary literature (see especially 1 Enoch 9:1; 20:1-8; 40:8-10; Luke 1:19, 26; Jude 9; and Rev 12:7).

These divine intermediaries may function in other ways than as messengers. Angels may carry out God's judgment on earth, as when the army of Sennacherib was destroyed (2 Kgs 19:35; Isa 37:36). Angels probably made up that army of the Lord, of which Josh 5:13-14 speaks. A related role was that of guide and protector for Israel (Exod 23:20, 33; 33:2). Each of these functions reappears with reference to the "men" in Dan 10–12, providing additional support for calling them angels, even though Daniel does not.

Another of Daniel's terms is "prince" (as in Josh 5:14), of Persia and of Greece. There is background in the Old Testament and literature near the time of Daniel for this concept of heavenly beings associated with specific nations. Deuteronomy 32:8-9 speaks of fixing the bounds of the peoples according to the number of the sons of God (in the Septuagint and a Qumran manuscript of Deuteronomy; the Masoretic Text reads "sons of Israel"). The idea seems to have been that a heavenly being is assigned to each nation, but Israel is associated directly with God. Sirach, shortly before Dan 10–12 was written, also commented, "He appointed a ruler for every nation, but Israel is the Lord's own portion" (Sir 17:17). *Jubilees* 15:31-32, perhaps a bit earlier than Daniel, speaks more explicitly of spirits appointed to lead nations astray, but of no angel or spirit over Israel since God alone is their ruler. Daniel differs from these texts in speaking of Michael as Israel's prince (12:1). The need for God to judge the nations for their crimes has thus been projected into spiritual realms in which heavenly beings who are subordinate to God but disobedient also deserve judgment. The idea appears as early as Isa 24:21 (difficult to date, but postexilic): "On that day the Lord will punish the host of heaven in heaven, and on earth the kings of the earth." These are the roots from which the demonology of apocalyptic and later speculation grew, but there is no sign of its development in Daniel.

This is one of the ways the Old Testament differs from the religious literature of Israel's neighbors. The religions of other cultures are filled with supernatural beings: a pantheon of greater and lesser deities, plus demons and beneficent spirits. In contrast, the Old Testament authors speak of "messengers" who serve as the one God's intermediaries, and whose supernatural qualities are seldom emphasized. They look like men, and a fair number of them are in fact simply human beings. Other heavenly beings (cherubim and seraphim) are mentioned only rarely. But with Daniel comes a glimpse of another world, populated by "princes," whose conflicts in heaven are mirrored on earth. Jewish and Christian literature from this time on will develop elaborate scenarios involving angels and demons. Was this a partial surrender, finally, to polytheism? Had life become so much more complex than it had been for ancient Israel that the one God seemed to require assistants—specialists to care for various parts of his world? And had the problem of evil—perhaps as personified in Antiochus IV Epiphanes—become so acute that a spiritual archenemy engaged in a long-standing battle with the forces of good seemed to be a necessary conception?

Those developments are often explained as the result of the influence of Zoroastrian religion because of obvious parallels; but having resisted similar influences earlier, why give in now, when in other respects Jewish commitment to monotheism was stronger than it had ever been?

The reason for raising these questions is to raise a question about the popularity of angelology in contemporary culture. It is not to question whether or not angels exist, but rather to ask why they, assuming they do exist, should be very important in Christian thought. It may be that some people find that the concept of one God, responsible for the entire cosmos, makes God seem rather remote and inaccessible. The people of ancient Mesopotamia would choose a minor deity for special devotion, thinking such a god would be more likely to be interested in them than a Marduk or an Enlil. Does the interest in guardian angels fulfill a similar sense of need? For Christians, access to God is offered through One who became one of us, Jesus Christ, who promised, "I am with you always, to the end of the age" (Matt 28:20). For believers, the New Testament's claims about the all-sufficiency of Christ have been validated in the experiences of many Christians, and yet for others something seems to be missing from what Christ does for them, and they find belief in the active presence of angels to be reassuring. The rather small role that angels play in both Testaments does raise a question about how prominent they ought to be in contemporary Christian thought. (For an appropriately cautious discussion, see Barth 1960, 451-52, 459-63.)

Israelite religion also differs from those of the surrounding cultures in its disinterest in speculation about life after death.

> If ever there was a religion which was *not* the mere psychic projection of human longing for bliss, it was the Old Testament faith of Israel. Here we find a people that lives with its God, and lives with him in an extraordinary intensity, without any idea of an eternal life which would one day solve all the problems which remain unsolved on earth. (Schweizer 1979, 139)

The widespread acceptance of the resurrection hope after the agonies of persecution in the second century BC is thus rather remarkable. This represents a new direction in Jewish thought concerning the state of the dead (Martin-Achard 1960). Almost all of the Old Testament conceives of the dead occupying Sheol—the universal grave—with no distinction being made between the righteous and the wicked. Sheol is seldom described, and usually in contexts referring to the deaths of foreigners; but it was a place of darkness, dust, and weakness (see Isa 14:9-11; Ezek 32:21-30; Ps 88; Job 3:17-19) from which there was no return (2 Sam 12:23). If one died in a good old age, death was thought to be natural and no cause for great anxiety; one could "die in peace" and lie down with one's ancestors (Gen 15:15; 35:29; Job 5:26). The worst thing about it was separation from worship in the community, so that one could no longer praise God (Pss 88:5, 10-12; 115:17). The death of a young person who died without children was truly tragic, however, and the cause of severe grief (e.g., Judg 11:37-40), but we find no evidence of measures taken to alleviate that grief in the Old Testament, except for the custom of levirate marriage. This was a legal fiction intended to provide an heir for a man who died childless, so that his name could live on (Deut 25:5-10).

There is thus very little in the Old Testament that points toward the affirmation in Dan 12:2. The Psalmists sometimes insisted that not even death could separate them from God (Pss 49:15; 73:24; 139:7-12), but these feelings do not develop into doctrine. The idea that there might be a life after death was known, since it was part of the beliefs of neighboring cultures, but both Job and Ecclesiastes considered it and rejected it for lack of evidence it might be true (Job 14; Eccl 3:19-22; 6:6). Very near to the time when Dan 12 was written, Sirach continued to assert that nothing but Sheol lies beyond death (14:16-19; 17:27-28).

Three elements of Israelite tradition lie behind the development of the resurrection hope, which became an accepted part of the Jewish faith (except for the Sadducees, Mark 12:18) remarkably soon after the date of the book of Daniel. Note 2 Macc 7:9, 14, 23, 29, written about 50 BC, and John 11:24. The first element is Hebrew anthropology. To be human means to have an animated body (Gen 2:7), and in the Old Testament there is no indication of an idea of disembodied humanity. The term *nepeš*, often translated "soul," is not something separable, as in Greek anthropology, but really means "person" (Wolff 1974, 10-28). For life after death to be meaningful life, then, it had to involve a body.

The second element was the insistence on the justice of God

that ruled Israelite thought, and the tendency to define justice with special reference to caring for those who could not care for themselves (e.g., Deut 10:17-19; Ps 146:7-9). Evidence that God does indeed rule the world justly was unfortunately not always obvious, and God could be challenged to "live up to his reputation," as in Hab 1. For a moment, Job even denied there is a just God (Job 24), but even he did not hold to that, and concluded his speeches with an affirmation that assumes justice still should prevail (Job 31). The sufferings of the martyrs under Antiochus IV put the belief in a just God to a severe test, however. Until that time, it might have been possible to try to explain anyone's sufferings as Job's "friends" had done: "Even though it may not be evident, you *must* have done something to deserve this." The persecution meant that it was precisely the most righteous who suffered the worst, while those who had given up the true faith (as Daniel saw it) were prospering. No concept of justice in this life could explain that, but divine justice continued to be affirmed with a new appeal to the old traditions of the power of God, even over death.

God is the source of all life; gives it and takes it away (1 Sam 2:6). As the one who gives life, he *could* even restore it after death, if God chose to do so. A few accounts of resuscitations thus appear in the Old Testament (1 Kgs 17:17-24; 2 Kgs 4:19-37; 13:21). Such rare events did not lead to hope for resurrection of everyone in the last days, and they were not in fact resurrections, for the people presumably died again, and stayed dead. When Ezekiel in a vision saw a valley strewn with dry bones and was asked, "Mortal, can these bones live?" he gave the correct answer: "O Lord GOD, you know" (Ezek 37:3). God *can* raise the dead if he chooses, but for Ezekiel and his people it was not an assumption that he would. And the vision does not speak of resurrection of individuals in the last days, although Christians, looking for the doctrine in the Old Testament, have frequently read it that way. The vision promises that Israel, which has lost its life in exile, will be restored: "These bones are the whole house of Israel" (Ezek 37:11). But Daniel has taken the bold step to affirm that the God who is the source of all life, who can restore life to the dead if he wishes, *will* raise the dead so that justice may be done.

For Judaism of this period resurrection was very much a justice issue, and the same seems to have been true of the earliest interpretations of Christ's resurrection appearances. He had died a shameful death, apparently under a curse (Gal 3:13; Deut 21:23), but his resurrection was vindication (Acts 2:24-32; 5:30-31). The belief that one man had already been raised from the dead to experience the new life that Jews hoped for in the last days provided a new and quite different basis for the Christian resurrection hope. It was now not a theological response to the need to be able to affirm the justice of God, but was a conclusion drawn from the fact that one resurrection had already occurred. So Paul argues at some length in 1 Cor 15. He makes it clear that he does not speak of resuscitation of the old body, but of a new creation, adding something to the Old Testament hopes for new creation (as in Isa 25:6-8; 35:5-7; 60:19-20; 65:17-25).

The promise in 1 John 3:2 leads to some additional reflections on the book of Daniel. "Beloved, we are God's children now; what we will be has not yet been revealed. What we do know is this: when he is revealed, we will be like him, for we will see him as he is." Daniel was a seer, but we have noticed that his visions all required explanation with words. And his visions—even the one in chapter 7—were concerned with life on earth. He made no effort to describe the life after death, except for the few allusive words in 12:3. As Eduard Schweizer wrote about 1 John 3:2, we hear now and will see then (Schweizer 1979, 137-38). Daniel knew that not much can be said about "then"; it is a matter of faith and hope, not of knowledge. But the Word gives us knowledge of what we must do now.

The apocalyptic literature has often been accused of quietism. For these writers, the powers of evil are too strong for human effort to accomplish anything. All the faithful can do is wait for divine intervention, so texts such as Dan 2:45 and 8:25 seem to indicate. The *maśkîlîm* have their work to do, we learn from chapters 11 and 12. It is their role to give understanding to many (11:33) and thus to justify the many ("lead many to righteousness," 12:3). Daniel has no interest in violent resistance, but spiritual resistance is essential, and that obviously calls for teaching and exemplary lives. That kind of resistance may lead to loss of life, but that is all right—not defeat after all (11:35; 12:1*b*-3). Even martyrdom can be accepted because of the certainty, which runs through the whole book, that God is sovereign. Under persecution, belief in the sovereignty of God meant personal certainty concerning two things: in spite of the present power of evil, God will ultimately triumph and establish righteousness on earth; and the God who gives all life cannot be defeated, even by the power of death.

SELECT BIBLIOGRAPHY

WORKS CITED IN THE TEXT

Alfrink, B. 1959. "L'idée de Résurrection d'après Dan. XII, 1.2." *Biblica* 40:355-71.

Allegro, John M. 1968. *Qumran Cave 4. I (4Q158–4Q186)*. Discoveries in the Judaean Desert V. Oxford: Clarendon Press.

Archer, Gleason L., Jr. (trans.). 1977. *Jerome's Commentary on Daniel*. Grand Rapids: Baker Book House.

Barth, Karl. 1960. *Church Dogmatics*. III, 3. The Doctrine of Creation. Edinburgh: T & T Clark.

Barton, George A. 1899/1900. "The Story of Ahikar and the Book of Daniel." *American Journal of Semitic Languages* 16:242-47.

Beaulieu, Paul-Alain. 1995. "King Nabonidus and the Neo-Babylonian Empire" in *Civilizations of the Ancient Near East*, ed. Jack M. Sasson, 2:969-79. New York: Scribner's.

Bickerman, Elias. 1967. *Four Strange Books of the Bible: Jonah/Daniel/Koheleth/Esther*. New York: Schocken Books.

_____. 1962. *From Ezra to the Last of the Maccabees: Foundations of Post-Biblical Judaism*. New York: Schocken Books.

Brekelmans, C. H. W. 1965. "The Saints of the Most High and Their Kingdom." *Oudtestamentische Studien* 14:305-29.

Caragounis, Chrys C. 1987. "The Interpretation of the Ten Horns of Daniel 7." *Ephemerides Theologicae Lovanienses* 63:106-12.

_____. 1993. "History and Supra-History: Daniel and the Four Empires" in *The Book of Daniel in the Light of New Findings*, ed. A. S. van der Woude. *Bibliotheca Ephemeridum Theologicarum Lovaniensium* 106:387-97. Leuven: University Press.

Casey, P. Maurice. 1979. *Son of Man. The Interpretation and Influence of Daniel 7*. London: SPCK.

Charles, R. H. 1913. *The Apocrypha and Pseudepigrapha of the Old Testament*. Oxford: Clarendon Press.

Collins, John J. 1977. *The Apocalyptic Vision of the Book of Daniel.* Harvard Semitic Monographs 16. Missoula, MT: Scholars Press.

_____. 1979. "Introduction: Towards the Morphology of a Genre." *Semeia* 14:1-19.

_____. 1984. *The Apocalyptic Imagination: An Introduction to the Jewish Matrix of Christianity.* New York: Crossroad.

_____. 1997. "Wisdom Reconsidered, in Light of the Scrolls." *Dead Sea Discoveries* 4:265-81.

Conybeare, F. C., J. R. Harris, and A. S. Lewis. 1913. *The Story of Ahikar.* Cambridge: Cambridge University Press.

Danthine, Helene. 1937. *Le palmier-dattier et les arbres sacrés sur les monuments de Mésopotamie et d'Élam.* Paris: P. Geuthner.

Davies, P. R. 1985. *Daniel. Old Testament Guides.* Sheffield: JSOR Press.

Delcor, M. 1993. "L'histoire selon le livre de Daniel, notament au chapitre XI" in *The Book of Daniel in the Light of New Findings,* ed. A. S. van der Woude. *Bibliotheca Ephemeridum Theologicarum Lovaniensium* 106:365-86. Leuven: University Press.

Di Lella, A. A. 1977. "The Holy One in Human Likeness and the Holy Ones of the Most High in Daniel 7." *Catholic Biblical Quarterly* 39:1-19.

Driver, G. R. 1963. "Sacred Figures and Round Numbers" in *Promise and Fulfillment: Essays Presented to Professor S. H. Hooke in Celebration of His Ninetieth Birthday,* ed. F. F. Bruce, 62-90. Edinburgh: T & T Clark.

Eliade, Mircea. 1958. *Patterns in Comparative Religion.* New York: Sheed & Ward.

Festinger, Leon, Henry W. Riecken, and Stanley Schachter. 1956. *When Prophecy Fails.* Minneapolis: University of Minnesota Press.

Fewell, Danna Nolan. 1988. *Circle of Sovereignty. A Story of Stories in Daniel 1–6.* Journal for the Study of the Old Testament Supplements 71; Bible and Literature Series 20. Sheffield: Almond Press.

Fitzmyer, Joseph A., S.J. 1995. *The Aramaic Inscriptions of Sefire,* rev. ed. Bibliotheca Orientalis 19A. Rome: Biblical Institute.

Gammie, John G. 1981. "On the Intention and Sources of Daniel I–VI." *Vetus Testamentum* 31:282-92.

Ginsberg, H. L. 1953. "The Oldest Interpretation of the Suffering Servant." *Vetus Testamentum* 3:400-4.

Gowan, Donald E. 1975. *When Man Becomes God: Humanism and Hybris in the Old Testament.* Pittsburgh Theological Monograph Series 6. Pittsburgh: Pickwick Press.

_____. 1992. "Reading Job as a 'Wisdom Script.' "*Journal for the Study of the Old Testament* 55:85-92.

_____. 2000. *Eschatology in the Old Testament.* 2d ed. Edinburgh: T & T Clark.

Grayson, A. K. 1975a. *Assyrian and Babylonian Chronicles.* Texts from Cuneiform Sources 5. Locust Valley, NY: J. J. Augustin Publisher.

_____. 1975b. *Babylonian Historical-Literary Texts.* Toronto Semitic Texts and Studies 3. Toronto: University of Toronto Press.

Humphreys, W. Lee. 1973. "A Lifestyle for Diaspora: A Study of the Tales of Esther and Daniel." *Journal of Biblical Literature* 92:211-23.

James, E. O. 1966. *The Tree of Life: An Archeological Study.* Leiden: Brill.

Jongeling, B., C. J. Labuschagne, and A. S. van der Woude. 1976. *Aramaic Texts from Qumran,* with translations and annotations. I. Semitic Study Series, n.s. IV. Leiden: Brill.

Kelso, James L. 1948. *The Ceramic Vocabulary of the Old Testament.* Bulletin of the American Schools of Oriental Research Supplements 5-6. New Haven: American Schools of Oriental Research.

Langdon, Stephen (ed.). 1905. *Building Inscriptions of the Neo-Babylonian Empire:* Part 1, Nabopolassar and Nebuchadnezzar. Paris: E. Leroux.

Lawson, Jack N. 1997. " 'The God Who Reveals Secrets': The Mesopotamian Background to Daniel 2.47." *Journal for the Study of the Old Testament* 74:61-76.

Lenglet, A. 1972. "La Structure littéraire de Daniel 2–7." *Biblica* 53:169-90.

Loud, Gordon. 1936. *Khorsabad.* Part 1. Oriental Institute Publications 38. Chicago: University of Chicago Press.

Martin-Achard, Robert. 1960. *From Death to Life: A Study of the Development of the Doctrine of the Resurrection in the Old Testament.* Edinburgh: Oliver & Boyd.

Mastin, B. A. 1973. "Daniel 2:46 and the Hellenistic World." *Zeitschrift für die Alttestamentliche Wissenschaft* 85:80-93.

Nickelsburgh, G. W. E. 1972. *Resurrection, Immortality, and Eternal Life in Intertestamental Judaism.* Harvard Theological Studies 26. Cambridge: Harvard University Press.

Niditch, Susan. 1983. *The Symbolic Vision in Biblical Tradition.* Harvard Semitic Monographs 30. Chico, CA: Scholars Press.

Niditch, Susan, and Robert Doran. 1977. "The Success Story of the Wise Courtier: A Formal Approach." *Journal of Biblical Literature* 96:179-93.

Noth, Martin. 1966a. "The Holy Ones of the Most High" in *The Laws in the Pentateuch and Other Studies*, 215-28. London: SCM Press.

_____. 1966b. "The Understanding of History in Old Testament Apocalyptic" in *The Laws in the Pentateuch and Other Studies*, 194-214. London: SCM Press.

Oppenheim, A. Leo. 1956. *The Interpretation of Dreams in the Ancient Near East*. Transactions of the American Philosophical Society, n.s. 3:179-373. Philadelphia: American Philosophical Society.

Parrot, André. 1961. *Nineveh and Babylon*. London: Thames & Hudson.

Pascal, Blaise. 1950. *Pascal's Pensées,* with an English translation, brief notes and introduction by H. F. Stewart. New York: Pantheon Books.

Perrot, Nell. 1937. *Les Représentations de L'Arbre Sacré sur les monuments de Mésopotamie et d'Elam.* Paris: Librairie Orientaliste Paul Geuthner.

Polak, F. H. 1993. "The Daniel Tales in Their Aramaic Literary Milieu" in *The Book of Daniel in the Light of New Findings,* ed. A. S. van der Woude. Bibliotheca Ephemeridum Theologicarum Lovaniensium 106:249-65. Leuven: University Press.

Porter, Paul A. 1983. *Metaphors and Monsters: A Literary-critical Study of Daniel 7 and 8.* Coniectania Biblica, Old Testament 20. Lund: Gleerup.

Pritchard, James B. (ed.). 1955. *Ancient Near Eastern Texts Relating to the Old Testament.* Princeton, NJ: Princeton University Press.

_____. 1969. *The Ancient Near East: Supplementary Texts and Pictures Relating to the Old Testament.* Princeton, NJ: Princeton University Press.

Pusey, E. B. 1868. *Daniel the Prophet.* Oxford: James Parker.

Reiner, Erica. 1958. *Shurpu: A Collection of Sumerian and Akkadian Incantations.* Graz: Archive für Orientforschung, 11.

Rowley, H. H. 1935. *Darius the Mede and the Four World Empires.* Cardiff: University of Wales Press.

Russell, Bertrand. 1938. *Power: A New Social Analysis.* New York: W. W. Norton.

Russell, D. S. 1964. *The Method and Message of Jewish Apocalyptic.* Philadelphia: Westminster Press.

Rylaarsdam, J. Coert. 1946. *Revelation in Jewish Wisdom Literature.* Chicago: University of Chicago Press.

Sayce, A. H. (ed.). 1890. *Records of the Past: Being English Translations of the Ancient Monuments of Egypt and Western Asia.* New Series, III. London: Samuel Bagster & Sons.

Schürer, Emil. 1973. *The History of the Jewish People in the Age of Jesus Christ* (175 BC–AD 135). A New English Edition, ed. Matthew Black. Edinburgh: T & T Clark.

Schweizer, Eduard. 1979. "Resurrection—Fact or Illusion?" *Horizons in Biblical Theology* 1:137-59.

Shea, William H. 1991. "Darius the Mede in His Persian-Babylonian Setting." *Andrews University Seminary Studies* 29:235-57.

Smith, George Adam. 1928. *The Book of Isaiah, I.* Garden City, NY: Doubleday, Doran & Company.

Swain, J. W. 1940. "The Theory of the Four Monarchies." *Classical Philology* 35:1-20.

Tcherikover, Victor. 1961. *Hellenistic Civilization and the Jews.* Philadelphia: Jewish Publication Society of America.

Torrey, Charles C. 1909. "Notes on the Aramaic Part of Daniel." *Transactions of the Connecticut Academy of Arts and Sciences* 15:241-82.

Towner, W. Sibley. 1983. "Were the English Puritans 'The Saints of the Most High'? Issues in the 'Pre-Critical' Interpretation of Daniel 7." *Interpretation* 37:46-63.

_____. 1985. "The Preacher in the Lions' Den." *Interpretation* 39:157-69. Reprinted in *Interpreting the Prophets*, ed. J. L. Mays and P. J. Achtemeier, 273-84. Philadelphia: Fortress Press.

Turville-Petre, E. O. G. 1964. *Myth and Religion of the North: The Religion of Ancient Scandanavia.* New York: Holt, Rinehart & Winston.

van der Woude, A. S. (ed.). 1993. *The Book of Daniel in the Light of New Findings.* Bibliotheca Ephemeridum Theologicarum Lovaniensium 106. Leuven: University Press.

Wenham, D. 1987. "The Kingdom of God and Daniel." *Expository Times* 98:132-34.

Wiseman, D. J. 1965. *Notes on Some Problems in the Book of Daniel.* London: Tyndale Press.

Wolff, Hans Walter. 1974. *Anthropology of the Old Testament.* Philadelphia: Fortress Press.

COMMENTARIES

Anderson, Robert A. 1984. *Signs and Wonders: A Commentary on the Book of Daniel.* International Theological Commentary. Grand

Rapids: Wm. B. Eerdmans Publishing Co.—A sound theological analysis of the book.

Charles, R. H. 1929. *A Critical and Exegetical Commentary on the Book of Daniel*. Oxford: Clarendon Press.—A thorough, philological study by one of the early specialists in apocalyptic literature, claiming superiority for the Greek version over the Masoretic Text, a position not widely held at present.

Collins, John J. 1993. *Daniel*. Hermeneia. Minneapolis: Fortress Press.—Very thorough, sound scholarship examining every possible parallel and including the history of interpretation, supplemented for the New Testament and postbiblical period by Adela Yarbro Collins.

Goldingay, John. 1989. *Daniel*. Word Biblical Commentary. Dallas: Word Books.—Of recent commentaries in English, second to Collins in thoroughness. More attention to the theology of the book.

Hartman, L. F. and A. Di Lella. 1978. *The Book of Daniel*. Anchor Bible. Garden City, NY: Doubleday.—Typical of the earlier Anchor Bible volumes; the focus is on history and philology.

Heaton, E. W. 1956. *The Book of Daniel*. Torch Bible Commentaries. London: SCM Press.—Brief, but with a relatively long introduction. Sound judgments often cited by other scholars.

Lacocque, André. 1979. *The Book of Daniel*. Atlanta: John Knox Press.—Original insights, not always well accepted by other commentators.

Miller, Stephen R. 1994. *Daniel*. The New American Commentary. Nashville: Broadman & Holman.—A recent advocate of the sixth-century date of the book.

Montgomery, James A. 1927. *A Critical and Exegetical Commentary on the Book of Daniel*. International Critical Commentary. Edinburgh: T & T Clark.—Still one of the most valuable studies of Daniel because of its philological detail and sound judgments.

Porteous, Norman W. 1965. *Daniel*. Old Testament Library. Philadelphia: Westminster Press.—Contains a theological essay on each chapter of the book.

Redditt, Paul L. 1999. *Daniel: Based on the New Revised Standard Version*. New Century Bible Commentary. Sheffield: Sheffield Academic Press.—Emphasizes the history of the composition of the book.

Smith-Christopher, Daniel L. 1966. "Daniel." *New Interpreter's Bible*, 7:17-152. Nashville: Abingdon Press.—A liberation-theology reading.

Towner, W. Sibley, 1984. *Daniel*. Interpretation: A Bible Commentary

for Teaching and Preaching. Atlanta: John Knox Press.—A sound theological reading of the book.

Young, E. J. 1949. *The Prophecy of Daniel*. Grand Rapids: Wm. B.
Eerdmans Publishing Co.—A thorough treatment of the text from a
conservative point of view. Useful example of the defense of the sixth-
century authorship.

INDEX

statue, 63, 65
Son of Man, 14, 16, 102, 105, 107-8, 110
symbolism, 30, 52, 103, 106, 110, 112, 122

temple, temple vessels, 42, 86, 92-93, 110, 116, 117-18, 120, 121, 126, 150, 151
Torah, 48-49, 136
tree (cosmic), 75-76, 78

violence, 115, 124, 150, 161

vision, 14, 15, 23, 29, 30-31, 36, 55, 61, 103, 105, 109, 113, 115-22, 132, 141, 152

wisdom, 25-27, 42, 50-52, 55, 59, 61, 63, 88, 92, 132, 150, 153-55
wisdom story, 25-27, 28, 59, 64, 87, 155
wise men, 25-26, 53, 61, 87

Zoroastrianism, 97, 157